First International Workshop on Social Threats in Online Conversations: Understanding and Management 2020

Marseille, France
11-16 May 2020

Editors:

Archna Bhatia
Samira Shaikh

ISBN: 978-1-7138-1278-4

Printed from e-media with permission by:

Curran Associates, Inc.
57 Morehouse Lane
Red Hook, NY 12571

Some format issues inherent in the e-media version may also appear in this print version.

Association for Computational Linguistics
209 N. Eighth Street
Stroudsburg, Pennsylvania 18360

Phone: 1-570-476-8006
Fax: 1-570-476-0860

acl@aclweb.org

Additional copies of this publication are available from:

Curran Associates, Inc.
57 Morehouse Lane
Red Hook, NY 12571 USA
Phone: 845-758-0400
Fax: 845-758-2633
Email: curran@proceedings.com
Web: www.proceedings.com

LREC 2020 Workshop
Language Resources and Evaluation Conference
11–16 May 2020

First International Workshop on Social Threats in Online Conversations: Understanding and Management

PROCEEDINGS

Editors:
Archna Bhatia and Samira Shaikh

Proceedings of the LREC 2020 First International Workshop on Social Threats in Online Conversations: Understanding and Management

Edited by: Archna Bhatia and Samira Shaikh

For more information:
European Language Resources Association (ELRA)
9 rue des Cordelières
75013, Paris
France
http://www.elra.info
Email: lrec@elda.org

Introduction

Welcome to the LREC 2020 Workshop on Social Threats in Online Conversations (STOC): Understanding and Management. The First STOC workshop was accepted to be held in conjunction with LREC 2020 (The 12th Edition of Language Resources and Evaluation Conference). Motivated by the need of using natural language processing (NLP) and computational sociolinguistics techniques in conjunction with metadata analysis, that can provide a better means for detecting and countering social engineering (SE) attacks and disinformation campaigns in a wide variety of online, conversational contexts, the main goal of the workshop was to glean actions and intentions of adversaries in online conversations, from the adversaries' language use coupled with communication content.

The organizing committee consisted of Archna Bhatia, Adam Dalton, Bonnie J. Dorr, Samira Shaikh and Tomek Strzałkowski. We solicited papers from a wide range of disciplines, including cybersecurity, NLP, computational sociolinguistics, Human-Computer Interaction and Psychology. We received a total of nine papers and accepted eight of these. Each paper was reviewed by at least three reviewers, two of the papers were reviewed by four reviewers to arrive at a decision.

The eight accepted papers dealt with a wide range of topics related to Social Threats online. In "The Panacea Threat Intelligence and Active Defense Platform", Dalton et al. describe a system that supports NLP components, including Ask and Framing detection, Named Entity Recognition, Dialogue Engineering and Stylometry for active defenses against SE attacks. The novelty of this system is in engaging the SE attacker using bots to waste the attacker's time and resources.

Bhatia et al. develop a paradigm for extensible lexical development based on Lexical Conceptual Structure in "Adaptation of a Lexical Organization for Social Engineering Detection and Response Generation". The paradigm supports resource extensions for new applications such as SE detection and response generation. Authors demonstrate that their proposed lexical organization refinements improve ask/framing detection and top ask identification, and yield qualitative improvements in response generation for defense from SE.

Kim et al. describe an automated approach to determine if a participant in online conversation is a cyberpredator in "Analysis of Online Conversations to Detect Cyberpredators Using Recurrent Neural Networks". Their experiments using recurrent neural networks on two datasets demonstrate that their approach provides better recall than prior, similar approaches.

Abeywardana and Thayasivam present their results to apply traditional structured privacy preserving techniques on unstructured data, including Twitter messages in their paper titled "A Privacy Preserving Data Publishing Middleware for Unstructured, Textual Social Media Data". They also make available a corpus of tweets that have been annotated for privacy related attributes.

In the paper "Information Space Dashboard", the authors Krumbiegel, Pritzkau and Schmitz created a dashboard that supports an analyst in generating a common operational picture of the information space, link it with an operational picture of the physical space and, thus, contribute to overarching situational awareness. They demonstrate their method on the analysis of historical data regarding violent anti-migrant protests and respective counter-protests that took place in Chemnitz in 2018.

Blackburn et al. in the paper "Corpus Development for Studying Online Disinformation Campaign: A Narrative + Stance Approach" discuss an end-to-end effort towards developing a corpus for studying disinformation campaigns across platforms, focusing on the Syrian White Helmets case study. They focused on the most challenging annotation tasks and an exploration of automated methods to extract narrative elements from microblogs.

Pascucci et al. describe their web service platform for disinformation detection in hotel reviews written in English in "Is this hotel review truthful or deceptive? A platform for disinformation detection through computational stylometry". Using the corpus of Deceptive Opinion Spam corpus, consisting of hotel reviews in four categories positive truthful, negative truthful, positive deceptive and negative deceptive reviews, the authors investigated four classifiers and demonstrated that Logistic Regression is the best performance algorithm for disinformation detection.

In "Email Threat Detection Using Distinct Neural Network Approaches", Castillo et al. use neural networks to detect malicious content in email interactions. Their goal is to obtain highly accurate detection of malicious emails based on email text alone. Their results show that back-propagation both with and without recurrent neural layers outperforms current state of the art techniques that include supervised learning algorithms with stylometric elements of texts as features.

The STOC workshop at LREC 2020 is cancelled due to Covid-19 pandemic, but these proceedings touch upon the research being conducted to study various dimensions of social threats in online conversations through techniques involving NLP, machine learning, computational sociolinguistics, and stylometry. We hope that this will provide a ground for future discussions and follow up workshops on topics related to social threats and SE.

Organizers:

Archna Bhatia, Institute for Human and Machine Cognition
Adam Dalton, Institute for Human and Machine Cognition
Bonnie J. Dorr, Institute for Human and Machine Cognition
Samira Shaikh, University of North Carolina at Charlotte
Tomek Strzalkowski, Rensselaer Polytechnic Institute

Program Committee:

Ehab Al-Shaer, UNCC
Genevieve Bartlett, USC-ISI
Emily Bender, U Washington
Larry Bunch, IHMC
Esteban Castillo, RPI
Dave DeAngelis, USC-ISI
Mona Diab, GWU/Google
Sreekar Dhaduvai, SUNY Albany
Min Du, UC Berkeley
Maxine Eskenazi, CMU
William Ferguson, Raytheon
Mark Finlayson, FIU
Marjorie Freedman, USC-ISI
Bryanna Hebenstreit, SUNY Albany
Christopher Hidey, Columbia
Scott Langevin, Uncharted
Christian Lebiere, CMU
Kristina Lerman, USC/ISI
Fei Liu, UCF
Amir Masoumzadeh, SUNY Albany
Kathleen McKeown, Columbia
Alex Memory, Leidos
Chris Miller, SIFT
Mark Orr, University of Virginia
Ian Perera, IHMC
Alan Ritter, OSU
Emily Grace Saldanha, PNNL
Sashank Santhanam, UNCC
Sonja Schmer-Galunder, SIFT
Svitlana Volkova, PNNL
Ning Yu, Leidos
Zhou Yu, UC Davis
Alan Zemel, SUNY Albany

Invited Speakers:

Rosanna E. Guadagno, Stanford University
Ian Harris, University of California Irvine

Table of Contents

Proceedings of the Workshop on Social Threats in Online Conversations: Understanding and Management (STOC-2020), pages 1–8
Language Resources and Evaluation Conference (LREC 2020), Marseille, 11–16 May 2020

Active Defense Against Social Engineering: The Case for Human Language Technology

Adam Dalton, Ehsan Aghaei, Ehab Al-Shaer, Archna Bhatia, Esteban Castillo, Zhuo Cheng, Sreekar Dhaduvai, Qi Duan, Bryanna Hebenstreit, Md Mazharul Islam, Younes Karimi, Amir Masoumzadeh, Brodie Mather, Sashank Santhanam, Samira Shaikh, Alan Zemel, Tomek Strzalkowski, Bonnie J. Dorr
IHMC, FL {adalton,abhatia,bmather,bdorr}@ihmc.us
SUNY Albany, NY {sdhaduvai,bhebenstreit,amasoumzadeh,ykarimi,azemel}@albany.edu
UNCC, NC {eaghaei,ealshaer,zcheng5,qduan,mislam7,ssantha1,sshaikh2}@uncc.edu
Rensselaer Polytechnic Institute, NY {castie2,tomek}@rpi.edu

Abstract

We describe Panacea, a system that supports natural language processing (NLP) components for active defenses against social engineering attacks. We deploy a pipeline of human language technology, including Ask and Framing Detection, Named Entity Recognition, Dialogue Engineering, and Stylometry. Panacea processes modern message formats through a plug-in architecture to accommodate innovative approaches for message analysis, knowledge representation and dialogue generation. The novelty of the Panacea system is that uses NLP for cyber defense and engages the attacker using bots to elicit evidence to attribute to the attacker and to waste the attacker's time and resources.

1 Introduction

Panacea (Personalized AutoNomous Agents Countering Social Engineering Attacks) actively defends against social engineering (SE) attacks. *Active* defense refers to engaging an adversary during an attack to extract and link attributable information while also wasting their time and resources in addition to preventing the attacker from achieving their goals. This contrasts with *passive* defenses, which decrease likelihood and impact of an attack (Denning, 2014) but do not engage the adversary.

SE attacks are formidable because intelligent adversaries exploit technical vulnerabilities to avoid social defenses, and social vulnerabilities to avoid technical defenses (Hadnagy and Fincher, 2015). A system must be socially aware to find attack patterns and indicators that span the socio-technical space. Panacea approaches this by incorporating the F3EAD (Find, Fix, Finish, Exploit, Analyze, and Disseminate) threat intelligence cycle (Gomez, 2011). The *find* phase identifies threats using language-based and message security approaches.The *fix* phase gathers relevant and necessary information to engage the adversaries and plan the mitigations that will prevent them from accomplishing their malicious goals. The *finish* phase performs a decisive and responsive action in preparation for the *exploit* phase for future attack detection. The *analysis* phase exploits intelligence from conversations with the adversaries and places it in a persistent knowledge base where it can be linked to other objects and studied additional context. The *disseminate* phase makes this intelligence available to all components to improve performance in subsequent attacks.

Panacea's value comes from NLP capabilities for cyber defense coupled with end-to-end plug-ins for ease of running NLP over real-world conversations. Figure 1 illustrates Panacea's active defense in the form of conversational engagement, diverting the attacker while also delivering a link that will enable the attacker's identity to be unveiled.

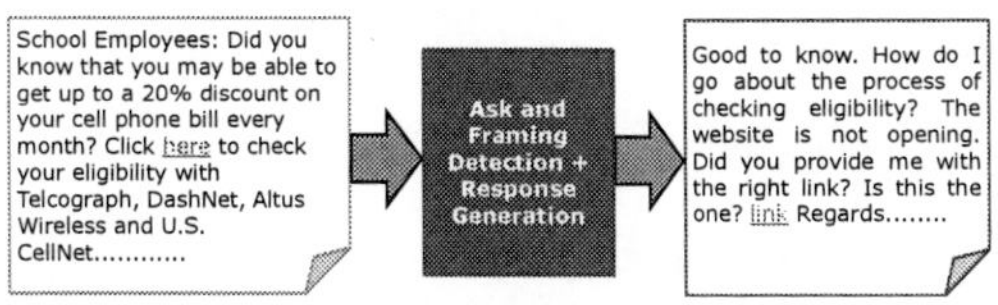

Figure 1: Active Defense against Social Engineering: Attacker's email (left) yields bot's response (right)

1.1 Use Cases

Panacea's primary use cases are: (1) monitoring a user's inbox to detect SE attacks; and (2) engaging the attacker to gain attributable information about their true identity while preventing attacks from succeeding. Active SE defense tightly integrates offensive and defensive capabilities to detect and respond to SE campaigns. Engaging the adversary uniquely enables extraction of indicators required to confidently classify a communication as malicious. Active defenses also carry significant risk because engagement can potentially harm an individual's or organization's reputation. Thus, high confidence classification is vital.

1.1.1 Monitoring and Detection

Panacea includes an initial protection layer based on the analysis of incoming messages. Conceptual users include end users and IT security professionals. Each message is processed and assigned a label of friend, foe, or unknown, taking into account headers and textual information of each message. The data obtained from this analysis is converted into threat intelligence and stored in a knowledge graph for use in subsequent phases, e.g., for meta analysis and message analysis in a broader context within a thread or in similar messages delivered to multiple users.

1.1.2 Engagement and Attribution

Passive defenses are finished once a threat is discovered, defused, and deconstructed; at this point Panacea's active defenses become engaged. Panacea's active defenses respond to the attacker's demands, reducing the risk that the attacker will catch on that they've been fingered. As such, any requests made by Panacea are more likely to be fulfilled by the attacker, bulwarked by hopes of eventual payoff. Such requests are implemented as a collection of flag seeking strategies built on top of a conversational theory of *asks*. Flags are collected using information extraction techniques. Future work includes inferential logic and deception detection to unmask an attacker and separate them from feigned identities used to gain trust.

2 Related Work

Security in online communication is a challenge due to: (1) attacker's speed outpacing that of defenders to maintain indicators (Zhang et al., 2006); (2) phishing site quality high enough that users ignore alerts (Egelman et al., 2008); (3) user training falling short as users forget material and fall prey to previously studied attacks (Caputo et al., 2013); the divergent goals of the attacker and defender (Li et al., 2020); and (4) defensive system maintainers who may ignore account context, motivations, and socio-economic status of the targeted user (Oliveira et al., 2017). Prior studies (Bakhshi et al., 2008; Karakasilitiosis et al., 2006) demonstrate human susceptibility to SE attacks. Moving from bots that detect such attacks to those that produce "natural sounding" responses, i.e., conversational agents that engage the attacker to elicit identifying information, is the next advance in this arena.

Prior work extracts information from email interactions (Dada et al., 2019), applies supervised learning to identify email signatures and forwarded messages (Carvalho and Cohen, 2004), and classifies email content into different structural sections (Lampert et al., 2009). Statistical and rule-based heuristics extract users' names and aliases (Yin et al., 2011) and structured script representations determine whether an email resembles a password reset email typically sent from an organization's IT department (Li and Goldwasser, 2019). Analysis of chatbot responses (Prakhar Gupta and Bigham, 2019) yields human-judgement correlation improvements. Approaches above differ from ours in that they require extensive model training.

Our approach relates to work on conversational agents, e.g., response generation using neural models (Gao et al., 2019; Santhanam and Shaikh, 2019), topic models (Dziri et al., 2018), self-disclosure for targeted responses (Ravichander and Black, 2018), topic models (Bhakta and Harris, 2015), and other NLP analysis (Sawa et al., 2016). All such approaches are limited to a pre-defined set of topics, constrained by the training corpus. Other prior work focuses on persuasion detection/prediction (Hidey and McKeown, 2018) but for judging when a persuasive attempt might be successful, whereas Panacea aims to achieve effective dialogue for countering (rather than adopting) persuasive attempts. Text-based semantic analysis is also used for SE detection (Kim et al., 2018), but not for *engaging* with an attacker. Whereas a bot might be employed to warn a potential victim that an attack is underway, our bots communicate with a social engineer in ways that elicit identifying information.

Panacea's architecture is inspired by state-of-the-art systems in cyber threat intelligence. MISP (Wagner et al., 2016) focuses on information sharing from a community of trusted organizations. MITRE's Collaborative Research Into Threats (CRITs) (Goffin, 2020) platform is, like Panacea, built on top of the Structured Threat Intelligence eXchange (STIX) specification. Panacea differs from these in that it is part of operational active defenses, rather than solely an analytical tool for incident response and threat reporting.

3 System Overview

Panacea's processing workflow is inspired by Stanford's CoreNLP annotator pipeline (Manning et al., 2014a), but with a focus on using NLP to power active defenses against SE. A F3EAD-inspired phased analysis and engagement cycle is employed to conduct active defense operations. The cycle is triggered when a message arrives and is deconstructed into STIX threat intelligence objects. Object instances for the identities of the sender and all recipients are found or created in the knowledge base. Labeled relationships are created between those identity objects and the message itself.

Once a message is ingested, plug-in components process the message in the *find* phase, yielding a response as a JSON object that is used by plug-in components in subsequent phases. Analyses performed in this phase include message part decomposition, named entity recognition, and email header analysis. The *fix* phase uses components dubbed *deciders*, which perform a meta-analysis of the results from the *find* phase to determine if and what type of an attack is taking place. *Ask detection* provides a fix on what the attacker is going after in the *fix* phase, if an attack is indicated. Detecting an attack advances the cycle to the *finish* phase, where response generation is activated.

Each time Panacea successfully elicits a response from the attacker, the new message is *exploited* for attributable information, such as the geographical location of the attack and what organizational affiliations they may have. This information is stored as structured intelligence in the knowledge base which triggers the *analysis* phase, wherein the threat is re-analyzed in a broader context. Finally, Panacea disseminates threat intelligence so that humans can build additional tools and capabilities to combat future threats.

4 Under the Hood

Panacea's main components are presented: (1) Message Analysis Component; and (2) Dialogue Component. The resulting system is capable of handling the thousands of messages a day that would be expected in a modern organization, including failure recovery and scheduling jobs for the future. Figure 2 shows Panacea throughput while operating over a one month backlog of emails, SMS texts, and LinkedIn messages.

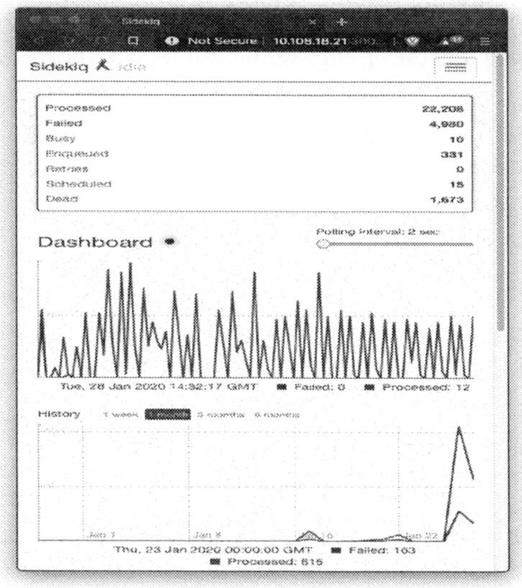

Figure 2: Panacea components run asynchronously in the background for scaling and so new components can be added and removed based on the underlying task.

4.1 Message Analysis Component

Below we describe the structural aspects of messages and their associated processing.

4.1.1 Email Header Classification

When communication takes place over a network, metadata is extracted that serves as a user fingerprint and a source for reputation scoring. Email headers, for example, contain authentication details and information about the mail servers that send, receive, and relay messages as they move from outbox to inbox. To distinguish between benign and malicious emails, Panacea applies a multistage email spoofing, spamming, and phishing detector consisting of: (1) a signature-based detector, (2) an active investigation detector, (3) a receiver-oriented anomaly detector, and (4) a sender-oriented anomaly detector.

4.1.2 Email Content Classification

Dissecting email headers is not enough for detecting malicious messages. Many suspicious elements are related to email bodies that contain user messages related to a specific topic and domain. Analyzing email content provides valuable insight for detecting threats in conversations and a solid understanding of the content itself. Panacea incorporates machine learning algorithms that, alongside of header classifiers, digest email exchanges:

Benign/non-benign classifier: Word embedding vectors (Bengio et al., 2006; Mikolov et al., 2013) trained on email samples from different companies (e.g., Enron) are extracted using neural networks (Sherstinsky, 2013), i.e., back-propagation model with average word vectors as features. This classifier provides a binary prediction regarding the nature of emails (friend or foe).

Email threat type classifier: Spam, phishing, malware, social-engineering and propaganda are detected, providing fine-grained information about the content of emails and support for motive detection (i.e., attacker's intention).

Email zone classifier: Greetings, body, and signature are extracted using word embedding implemented as recurrent neural network with handcrafted rules, thus yielding senders, receivers and relevant entities to enable response generation.

All classifiers support active detection of malicious emails and help in the engagement process of automated bots. Additionally, all trained models have an overall accuracy of 90% using a cross validation approach against well known email collections like Enron (Klimt and Yang, 2004) and APWG (Oest et al., 2018) among other non-public datasets, which makes them reasonably reliable in the context of passive defenses.

4.1.3 Behavioral Modeling

If an adversary is able to compromise a legitimate account, then the header and content classifiers will not be sufficient to detect an attack. The social engineer is able to extract contacts of the account owner and send malicious content on their behalf, taking advantage of the reputation and social relationships attributed to the hijacked account. Two distinctive approaches address these issues:

Impersonation Detector: Sender entities are extracted from the email message and a personalized profile is created for each one, with communication habits, stylometric features, and social network. The unique profiled model is used to assess whether this email has been written and sent by an account's legitimate owner. If a message arrives from a sender that does not have a profile, Panacea applies similarity measures to find other email addresses for the unknown entity. This serves as a defense against impersonation attacks where the social engineer creates an email account using a name and address similar to the user of an institutional account for which a model is available. If Panacea links the unknown account to an institutional account, then that account's model is used to determine whether a legitimate actor is using an unknown account, or a nefarious actor is attempting to masquerade as an insider in order to take advantage of the access such an account would have.

Receiving Behavior Classifier. Individual profiles are built for the receiving behavior of each entity (how and with whom this entity communicates) and new emails are evaluated against the constructed models. To build unique profiles, all messages sent to each particular entity are collected.

4.1.4 Deciders

Panacea must have high confidence in determining that a message is coming from an attacker before deploying active defense mechanisms. A strategy-pattern approach fits different meta-classifiers to different situations. Four classification strategies, called *Deciders*, combine all component analyses after a message is delivered to an inbox to make the final *friend/foe* determination. The Decider API expects all component analyses to include a *friend/foe* credibility score using six levels defined by the Admiralty Code (JDP 2-00, 2011). Deciders may be deterministic through the application of rule based decision making strategies or they may be trained to learn to identify threats based on historical data.

4.1.5 Threat Intelligence

Panacea stores component analysis results in a threat intelligence knowledge base for aggregation of attack campaigns with multiple turns, targets, and threads. The knowledge base adheres to STIX 2.0 specifications and implements MITRE's ATT&CK framework (Strom et al., 2017) to enable attribution and anticipatory mitigations of sophisticated SE attacks. Panacea recognizes indicators of compromise based on features of individual emails as well as historical behavior of senders and recipients. Intrusion sets and campaigns are thus constructed when malicious messages are discovered subsequently linked to threat actors based on attribution patterns, such as IP address, message templates, socio-behavioral indicators, and linguistic signatures. This feature set was prioritized to work with Unit 42's ATT&CK Playbook Viewer. The knowledge base uses a PostgreSQL database backend with an application layer built with Ruby on Rails.

4.2 Dialogue Component

Panacea's dialogue component consists of three key sub-components: *Ask/Framing Detection* (to determine the attacker's demand), *Motive Detection* (to determine the attacker's goal), and **Response Generation** (to reply to suspicious messages).

4.2.1 Ask/Framing Detection

Once an email is processed as described above, linguistic knowledge and structural knowledge are used to extract candidate Ask/Framing pairs and to provide the final confidence-ranked output.

Application of Linguistic Knowledge: Linguistic knowledge is employed to detect both the *ask* (e.g., buy gift card) and the *framing* (e.g., lose your job, get a 20% discount). An ask may be, for example, a request for something (GIVE) or an action (PERFORM). On the other hand, framing may be a reward (GAIN) or a risk (LOSE), for example. Ask/framing detection relies on Stanford CoreNLP constituency parses and dependency trees (Manning et al., 2014b), coupled with *semantic role labeling* (SRL) (Gardner et al., 2017), to identify the main action and arguments. For example, *click here* yields *click* as the *ask* and its argument *here*.

Additional constraints are imposed through the use of a lexicon based on Lexical Conceptual Structure (LCS) (Dorr and Olsen, 2018; Dorr and Voss, 2018), derived from a pool of team members' collected suspected scam/impersonation emails. Verbs from these emails were grouped as follows:

- PERFORM: connect, copy, refer
- GIVE: administer, contribute, donate
- LOSE: deny, forget, surrender
- GAIN: accept, earn, grab, win

Additional linguistic processing includes: (1) categorial variation (Habash and Dorr, 2003) to map between different parts of speech, e.g., *reference*(N) → *refer*(V) enables detection of an explicit ask from *you can reference your gift card*; and (2) verbal processing to eliminate spurious asks containing verb forms such as *sent* or *signing* in *sent you this email because you are signing up*.

Application of Structural Knowledge: Beyond meta-data processing described previously, the email body is further pre-processed before linguistic elements are analyzed. Lines are split where `div`, `p`, `br`, or `ul` tags are encountered. Placeholders are inserted for hyperlinks. Image tags are replaced with their alt text. All styling, scripting, quoting, replying, and signature are removed.

Social engineers employ different link positionings to present "click bait," e.g., "Click here" or "Contact me (jw11@example.com)." Basic link processing assigns the link to the appropriate ask (e.g., *click here*). Advanced link processing ties together an email address with its corresponding PERFORM ask (e.g., *contact me*), even if separated by intervening material.

Confidence Score and Top Ask: Confidence scores are heuristically assigned: (1) Past tense events are assigned low or 0 confidence; (2) The vast majority of asks associated with URLs (e.g., jw11@example.com) are found to be PERFORM asks with highest confidence (0.9); (3) a GIVE ask combined with any ask category (e.g., *contribute $50*) is less frequently found to be an ask, thus assigned slightly lower confidence (0.75); and (4) GIVE by itself is even less likely found to be an ask, thus assigned a confidence of 0.6 (e.g., *donate often*). Top ask selection then selects highest confidence asks at the aggregate level of a single email. This is crucial for downstream processing, i.e., response generation in the dialogue component. For example, the ask "PERFORM contact (jw11@example.com)" is returned as the top ask for "*Contact me. (jw11@example.com).*"

4.2.2 Motive Detection

In addition to the use of distinct tools for detecting linguistic knowledge, Panacea extracts the attacker's intention, or *motive*. Leveraging the attacker's demands (asks), goals (framings) and message attack types (from the threat type classifier), the Motive Detection module maps to a range of possible motive labels: *financial information*, *acquire personal information*, *install malware*, *annoy recipient*, etc. Motive detection maps to such labels from top asks/framings and their corresponding threat types. Examples are shown here:

$$\underbrace{\textit{Give}}_{\text{Ask}} + \underbrace{\textit{Finance info}}_{\text{Ask type}} + \underbrace{\textit{Spam}}_{\text{Email threat}} \rightarrow \textit{Financial info}$$

$$\underbrace{\textit{Gain}}_{\text{Framing}} + \underbrace{\textit{Credentials}}_{\text{Ask type}} + \underbrace{\textit{Malware}}_{\text{Email threat}} \rightarrow \textit{Install malware}$$

These motives are used later for enhancing a response generation process which ultimately creates automatic replies for all malicious messages detected in the Panacea platform.

4.2.3 Response Generation

Response generation is undertaken by a bot using templatic approach to yield appropriate responses based on a hierarchical attack ontological structure and ask/framing components. The hierarchical ontology contains 13 major categories (e.g., *financial details*). Responses focus on wasting the attacker's time or trying to gain information from the attacker while moving along *F3EAD* threat intelligence cycle (Gomez, 2011) to ensure that the attacker is kept engaged. The response generation focuses on the *find, finish and exploit* states. The bot goes after name, organization, location, social media handles, financial information, and is also capable of sending out malicious links that obtain pieces of information about the attacker's computer.

A dialogue state manager decides between time wasting and information seeking based on motive, ontological structure and associated ask/framing of the message. For example, if an attack message has motive *financial details* and ontological structure of *bank information*, coupled with a PERFORM ask, the dialogue state manager moves into an information gathering phase and produces this response: "*Can you give me the banking information for transferring money? I would need the bank name, account number and the routing information. This would enable me to act swiftly.*" On the other hand if the attacker is still after financial information but not a particular piece of information, the bot wastes time, keeping the attacker in the loop.

5 Evaluation

Friend/foe detection (Message Analysis) and response generation (Dialogue) are evaluated for effectiveness of Panacea as an effective intermediary between attackers and potential victims.

5.1 Message Analysis Module

The DARPA ASED program evaluation tests header and content modules against messages for friend/foe determination. Multiple sub-evaluations check system accuracy in distinguishing malicious messages from benign ones, reducing the false alarm rate, and transmitting appropriate messages to dialogue components for further analysis. Evaluated components yield ~90% accuracy. Components adapted for detecting borderline exchanges (*unknown* cases) are shown to help dialogue components request more information for potentially malicious messages.

5.2 Dialogue Module

The ASED program evaluation also tests the dialogue component. Independent evaluators communicate with the system without knowledge of whether they are interacting with humans or bots. Their task is to engage in a dialogue for as many turns as necessary. Panacea bots are able to sustain conversations for an average of 5 turns (across 15 distinct threads). Scoring applied by independent evaluators yield a rating of 1.9 for their ability to display human-like communication (on a scale of 1–3; 1=bot, 3=human). This score is the highest amongst all other competing approaches (four other teams) in this independent program evaluation.

6 Conclusions and Future Work

Panacea is an operational system that processes communication data into actionable intelligence and provides active defense capabilities to combat SE. The F3EAD active defense cycle was chosen because it fits the SE problem domain, but specific phases could be changed to address different problems. For example, a system using the Panacea processing pipeline could ingest academic papers on a disease, process them with components designed to extract biological mechanisms, then engage with paper authors to ask clarifying questions and search for additional literature to review, while populating a knowledge base containing the critical intelligence for the disease of interest.

Going forward, the plan is to improve Panacea's plug-in infrastructure so that it is easier to add capability without updating Panacea itself. This is currently possible as long as new components use the same REST API as existing components. The obvious next step is to formalize Panacea's API. We have found value to leaving it open at this early state of development as we discover new challenges and solutions to problems that emerge in building a large scale system focused on the dangers and opportunities in human language communication.

Acknowledgments

This work was supported by DARPA through AFRL Contract FA8650-18- C-7881 and Army Contract W31P4Q-17-C-0066. All statements of fact, opinion or conclusions contained herein are those of the authors and should not be construed as representing the official views or policies of DARPA, AFRL, Army, or the U.S. Government.

References

Taimur Bakhshi, Maria Papadaki, and Steven Furnell. 2008. A practical assessment of social engineering vulnerabilities. In *Proceedings of the Second International Symposium on Human Aspects of Information Security & Assurance.*

Yoshua Bengio, Holger Schwenk, Jean-Sébastien Senécal, Fréderic Morin, and Jean-Luc Gauvain. 2006. *Neural Probabilistic Language Models*, pages 137–186. Springer Berlin Heidelberg, Berlin, Heidelberg.

Ram Bhakta and Ian G. Harris. 2015. Semantic analysis of dialogs to detect social engineering attacks. *Proceedings of the 2015 IEEE 9th International Conference on Semantic Computing (IEEE ICSC 2015)*, pages 424–427.

Deanna D Caputo, Shari Lawrence Pfleeger, Jesse D Freeman, and M Eric Johnson. 2013. Going spear phishing: Exploring embedded training and awareness. *IEEE Security & Privacy*, 12(1):28–38.

Vitor Carvalho and William Cohen. 2004. Learning to extract signature and reply lines from email. In *First Conference on Email and Anti-Spam*, pages 1–8. CEAS.

Emmanuel G. Dada, Joseph S. Bassi, Haruna Chiroma, Shafi'i M. Abdulhamid, Adebayo O. Adetunmbi, and Opeyemi E. Ajibuwa. 2019. Machine learning for email spam filtering: review, approaches and open research problems. *Heliyon*, 5(6):1–23.

Dorothy E. Denning. 2014. Framework and principles for active cyber defense. *Computers & Security*, 40:108–113.

Bonnie Dorr and Clare Voss. 2018. STYLUS: A resource for systematically derived language usage. In *Proceedings of the First Workshop on Linguistic Resources for Natural Language Processing*, pages 57–64, Santa Fe, New Mexico, USA. Association for Computational Linguistics.

Bonnie J. Dorr and Mari Broman Olsen. 2018. Lexical conceptual structure of literal and metaphorical spatial language: A case study of push. In *Proceedings of the First International Workshop on Spatial Language Understanding*, pages 31–40.

Nouha Dziri, Ehsan Kamalloo, Kory W Mathewson, and Osmar Zaiane. 2018. Augmenting neural response generation with context-aware topical attention. *arXiv preprint arXiv:1811.01063*.

Serge Egelman, Lorrie Faith Cranor, and Jason Hong. 2008. You've been warned: An empirical study of the effectiveness of web browser phishing warnings. In *Proceedings of the SIGCHI Conference on Human Factors in Computing Systems*, CHI '08, pages 1065–1074, New York, NY, USA. ACM.

Jianfeng Gao, Michel Galley, Lihong Li, et al. 2019. Neural approaches to conversational ai. *Foundations and Trends in Information Retrieval*, 13(2-3):127–298.

Matt Gardner, Joel Grus, Mark Neumann, Oyvind Tafjord, Pradeep Dasigi, Nelson F. Liu, Matthew Peters, Michael Schmitz, and Luke S. Zettlemoyer. 2017. Allennlp: A deep semantic natural language processing platform. In *Proceedings of Workshop for NLP Open Source Software (NLP-OSS)*.

Mike Goffin. 2020. CRITs - Collaborative Research Into Threats.

Jimmy A. Gomez. 2011. The targeting process: D3A and F3EAD. *Small Wars Journal*, 1:1–17.

Nizar Habash and Bonnie J. Dorr. 2003. A categorial variation database for english. In *In Proceedings of the Human Language Technology and North American Association for Computational Linguistics (NAACL) Conference*, pages 96–102.

Christopher Hadnagy and Michele Fincher. 2015. *Phishing Dark Waters*. Wiley Online Library.

Christopher Hidey and Kathleen McKeown. 2018. Persuasive Influence Detection: The Role of Argument Sequencing. In *Proceedings of the Thirty-Second AAAI Conference on Artificial Intelligence*, pages 5173–5180, San Francisco, California, USA.

JDP 2-00. 2011. *Understanding and intelligence support to joint operations (JDP 2-00)*. Ministry of Defence (UK).

A. Karakasilitiosis, S. M. Furnell, and M. Papadaki. 2006. Assessing end-user awareness of social engineering and phishing. In *Proceedings of the Australian Information Warfare and Security Conference*.

Myeongsoo Kim, Changheon Song, Hyeji Kim, Deahyun Park, Yeeji Kwon, Eun Namkung, Ian G Harris, and Marcel Carlsson. 2018. Catch me, yes we can!-pwning social engineers using natural language processing techniques in real-time.

Bryan Klimt and Yiming Yang. 2004. The enron corpus: A new dataset for email classification research. In *Machine Learning: ECML 2004*, pages 217–226. Springer Berlin Heidelberg.

Andrew Lampert, Robert Dale, and C'ecile Paris. 2009. Segmenting email message text into zones. In *Proceedings of the 2009 Conference on Empirical Methods in Natural Language Processing*, page 919–928. Association for Computational Linguistics.

Chang Li and Dan Goldwasser. 2019. Encoding social information with graph convolutional networks forPolitical perspective detection in news media. In *Proceedings of the 57th Annual Meeting of the Association for Computational Linguistics*, pages 2594–2604, Florence, Italy. Association for Computational Linguistics.

Yu Li, Kun Qian, Weiyan Shi, and Zhou Yu. 2020. End-to-end trainable non-collaborative dialog system. *ArXiv*, abs/1911.10742.

Christopher D. Manning, Mihai Surdeanu, John Bauer, Jenny Finkel, Steven J. Bethard, and David McClosky. 2014a. The Stanford CoreNLP natural language processing toolkit. In *Association for Computational Linguistics (ACL) System Demonstrations*, pages 55–60. ACL.

Christopher D. Manning, Mihai Surdeanu, John Bauer, Jenny Finkel, Steven J. Bethard, and David McClosky. 2014b. The Stanford CoreNLP natural language processing toolkit. In *Association for Computational Linguistics (ACL) System Demonstrations*, pages 55–60.

Tomas Mikolov, Ilya Sutskever, Kai Chen, Greg Corrado, and Jeffrey Dean. 2013. Distributed representations of words and phrases and their compositionality. In *Proceedings of the 26th International Conference on Neural Information Processing Systems - Volume 2*, pages 3111–3119. Curran Associates Inc.

Adam Oest, Yeganeh Safei, Adam Doupe, Gail-Joon Ahn, Brad Wardman, and Gary Warner. 2018. Inside a phisher's mind: Understanding the anti-phishing ecosystem through phishing kit analysis. In *Proceedings of the 2018 APWG Symposium on Electronic Crime Research, eCrime 2018*, pages 1–12. IEEE Computer Society.

Daniela Oliveira, Harold Rocha, Huizi Yang, Donovan Ellis, Sandeep Dommaraju, Melis Muradoglu, Devon Weir, Adam Soliman, Tian Lin, and Natalie Ebner. 2017. Dissecting spear phishing emails for older vs young adults: On the interplay of weapons of influence and life domains in predicting susceptibility to phishing. In *Proceedings of the 2017 CHI Conference on Human Factors in Computing Systems*, CHI '17, pages 6412–6424, New York, NY, USA. ACM.

Tiancheng Zhao Amy Pavel Maxine Eskenazi Prakhar Gupta, Shikib Mehri and Jeffrey Bigham. 2019. Investigating evaluation of open-domain dialogue systems with human generated multiple references. In *Proceedings of the 20th Annual Meeting of the Special Interest Group on Discourse and Dialogue*, Stockholm, Sweden. Association for Computational Linguistics.

Abhilasha Ravichander and Alan W. Black. 2018. An empirical study of self-disclosure in spoken dialogue systems. In *Proceedings of the 19th Annual SIGdial Meeting on Discourse and Dialogue, Melbourne, Australia, July 12-14, 2018*, pages 253–263.

Sashank Santhanam and Samira Shaikh. 2019. A survey of natural language generation techniques with a focus on dialogue systems-past, present and future directions. *arXiv preprint arXiv:1906.00500*.

Yuki Sawa, Ram Bhakta, Ian Harris, and Christopher Hadnagy. 2016. Detection of social engineering attacks through natural language processing of conversations. In *Proceedings of the 2016 IEEE Tenth International Conference on Semantic Computing (ICSC)*, pages 262–265.

Alex Sherstinsky. 2013. Fundamentals of recurrent neural network (rnn) and long short-term memory (lstm) network. pages 1–39. Cornell University.

Blake E. Strom, Joseph A. Battaglia, Michael S. Kemmerer, William Kupersanin, Douglas P. Miller, Craig Wampler, Sean M. Whitley, and Ross D. Wolf. 2017. Finding cyber threats with att&ck-based analytics. *The MITRE Corporation, Tech. Rep.*, 1(1).

Cynthia Wagner, Alexandre Dulaunoy, Gérard Wagener, and Andras Iklody. 2016. Misp: The design and implementation of a collaborative threat intelligence sharing platform. In *Proceedings of the 2016 ACM on Workshop on Information Sharing and Collaborative Security*, pages 49–56. ACM.

Meijuan Yin, Xiao Li, Junyong Luo, Xiaonan Liu, and Yongxing Tan. 2011. Automatically extracting name alias of user from email. *International Journal of Engineering and Manufacturing*, 1:14–24.

Yue Zhang, Serge Egelman, Lorrie Faith Cranor, and Jason I. Hong. 2006. Phinding phish: Evaluating anti-phishing tools. Technical report, Carnegie Mellon University.

Proceedings of the Workshop on Social Threats in Online Conversations: Understanding and Management (STOC-2020), pages 9–14
Language Resources and Evaluation Conference (LREC 2020), Marseille, 11–16 May 2020

Adaptation of a Lexical Organization for Social Engineering Detection and Response Generation

Archna Bhatia, Adam Dalton, Brodie Mather, Sashank Santhanam, Samira Shaikh, Alan Zemel, Tomek Strzalkowski, Bonnie J. Dorr
The Florida Institute for Human and Machine Cognition, The University of North Carolina at Charlotte, University of Albany NY, Rensselaer Polytechnic Institute NY
{abhatia,adalton,bmather,bdorr}@ihmc.us, {ssantha1,sshaikh2}@uncc.edu, azemel@albany.edu, tomek@rpi.edu

Abstract

We present a paradigm for extensible lexicon development based on Lexical Conceptual Structure to support social engineering detection and response generation. We leverage the central notions of *ask* (elicitation of behaviors such as providing access to money) and *framing* (risk/reward implied by the ask). We demonstrate improvements in ask/framing detection through refinements to our lexical organization and show that response generation qualitatively improves as ask/framing detection performance improves. The paradigm presents a systematic and efficient approach to resource adaptation for improved task-specific performance.

Keywords: resource adaptation, social engineering detection, response generation, NLP based bots for cyber defense

1. Introduction

Social engineering (SE) refers to sophisticated use of deception to manipulate individuals into divulging confidential or personal information for fraudulent purposes. Standard cybersecurity defenses are ineffective because attackers attempt to exploit humans rather than system vulnerabilities. Accordingly, we have built a *user alter-ego* application that detects and engages a potential attacker in ways that expose their identity and intentions.

Our system relies on a paradigm for extensible lexicon development that leverages the central notion of *ask*, i.e., elicitation of behaviors such as PERFORM (e.g., clicking a link) or GIVE (e.g., providing access to money). This paradigm also enables detection of risk/reward (or LOSE/GAIN) implied by an ask, which we call *framing* (e.g., *lose your job, get a raise*). These elements are used for countering attacks through bot-produced responses and actions. The system is tested in an email environment, but is applicable to other forms of online communications, e.g., SMS.

Email	Ask	Framing
(a) It is a pleasure to inform you that you have won 1.7Eu. Contact me. (jw11@example.com)	PERFORM contact (jw11@...)	GAIN won (1.7Eu)
(b) You won $1K. Did you send money? Do that by 9pm or lose money. Respond asap.	GIVE send (money)	LOSE lose (money)
(c) Get 20% discount. Check eligibility or paste this link: http.... Sign up for email alerts.	PERFORM paste (http...)	GAIN get (20%)

Table 1: LCS+ Ask/Framing output for three SE emails

More formally, an *ask* is a statement that elicits a behavior from a potential victim, e.g., *please buy me a gift card.* Although asks are not always explicitly stated (Drew and Couper-Kuhlen, 2014; Zemel, 2017), we discern these through navigation of semantically classified verbs. The task of ask detection specifically is targeted event detection based on parsing and/or Semantic Role Labeling (SRL), to identify semantic class triggers (Dorr et al., 2020). *Framing* sets the stage for the ask, i.e., the purported threat (LOSE) or benefit (GAIN) that the social engineer wants the potential victim to believe will obtain through compliance or lack thereof. It should be noted that there is no one-to-one ratio between ask and framing in the ask/framing detection output. Given the content, there may be none, one or more asks and/or framings in the output.

Our lexical organization is based on *Lexical Conceptual Structure* (LCS), a formalism that supports resource construction and extensions to new applications such as SE detection and response generation. Semantic classes of verbs with similar meanings (*give, donate*) are readily augmented through adoption of the STYLUS variant of LCS (Dorr and Voss, 2018) and (Dorr and Olsen, 2018). We derive LCS+ from asks/framings and employ CATVAR (Habash and Dorr, 2003) to relate word variants (e.g., *reference* and *refer*). Table 1 illustrates LCS+ Ask/Framing output for three (presumed) SE emails: two PERFORM asks and one GIVE ask.[1] Parentheses () refer to ask *arguments*, often a link that the potential victim might choose to click. Ask/framing outputs are provided to downstream response generation. For example, a possible response for Table 1(a) is *I will contact asap.*

A comparison of LCS+ to two related resources shows that our lexical organization supports refinements, improves ask/framing detection and top ask identification, and yields qualitative improvements in response generation. LCS+ is

[1] To view our system's ask/framing outputs on a larger dataset (the same set of emails which were also used for ground truth (GT) creation described below), refer to `https://social-threats.github.io/panacea-ask-detection/data/case7LCS+AskDetectionOutput.txt`.

deployed in a SE detection and response generation system. Even though LCS+ is designed for the SE domain, the approach to development of LCS+ described in this paper serves as a guideline for developing similar lexica for other domains. Correspondingly, even though development of LCS+ is one of the contributions of this paper, the main contribution is not this resource but the systematic and efficient approach to resource adaptation for improved task-specific performance.

2. Method

In our experiments described in Section 3., we compare LCS+, our lexical resource we developed for the SE domain, against two strong baselines: STYLUS and Thesaurus.

STYLUS baseline: As one of the baselines for our experiments, we leverage a publicly available resource STYLUS that is based on Lexical Conceptual Structure (LCS) (Dorr and Voss, 2018) and (Dorr and Olsen, 2018). The LCS representation is an underlying representation of spatial and motion predicates (Jackendoff, 1983; Jackendoff, 1990; Dorr, 1993), such as *fill* and *go*, and their metaphorical extensions, e.g., temporal (the hour *flew* by) and possessional (he *sold* the book).[2] Prior work (Jackendoff, 1996; Levin, 1993; Olsen, 1994; Chang et al., 2007; Chang et al., 2010; Kipper et al., 2007; Palmer et al., 2017) has suggested that there is a close relation between underlying lexical-semantic structures of verbs and nominal predicates and their syntactic argument structure. We leverage this relationship to extend the existing STYLUS verb classes for the resource adaptation to SE domain through creation of LCS+ which is discussed below.

For our STYLUS verb list, we group verbs into four lists based on asks (PERFORM, GIVE) and framings (LOSE, GAIN). The STYLUS verb list can be accessed here: `https://social-threats.github.io/panacea-ask-detection/resources/original_lcs_classes_based_verbsList.txt`. Examples of this classificationare shown below (with total verb count in parentheses):

- PERFORM (214): remove, redeem, refer
- GIVE (81): administer, contribute, donate
- LOSE (615): penalize, stick, punish, ruin
- GAIN (49): accept, earn, grab, win

Assignment of verbs to these four ask/framing categories is determined by a computational linguist, with approximately a person-day of human effort. Identification of genre-specific verbs is achieved through analysis of 46 emails (406 clauses) after parsing/POS/SRL is applied.

As an example, the verb *position* (Class 9.1) and the verb *delete* (Class 10.1) both have an underlying *placement* or *existence* component with an affected object (e.g., the cursor in *position your cursor* or the account in *delete your account*), coupled with a location (e.g., *here* or *from the system*). Accordingly, *Put* verbs in Class 9.1 and *Remove* verbs in Class 10.1 are grouped together and aligned with a PERFORM ask (as are many other classes with similar properties: Banish, Steal, Cheat, Bring, Obtain, etc.). Analogously, verbs in the *Send* and *Give* classes are aligned with a GIVE ask, as all verbs in these two classes have a sender/giver and a recipient.

Lexical assignment of framings is handled similarly, i.e., verbs are aligned with LOSE and GAIN according to their argument structures and components of meaning. It is assumed that the potential victim of a SE attack serves to lose or gain something, depending on non-compliance or compliance with a social engineer's ask. As an example, the framing associated with the verb *losing* (Class 10.5) in *Read carefully to avoid **losing** account access* indicates the risk of losing access to a service; Class 10.5 is thus aligned with LOSE. Analogously, the verb *win* (Class 13.5.1) in *You have **won** 1.7M Eu.* is an alluring statement with a purported gain to the potential victim; thus Class 13.5.1 is aligned with GAIN. In short, verbs in classes associated with LOSE imply negative consequences (Steal, Impact by Contact, Destroy, Leave) whereas verbs in classes associated with GAIN imply positive consequences (Get, Obtain).

Some classes are associated with more than one ask/framing category: Steal (Class 10.5) and Cheat (Class 10.6) are aligned with both PERFORM (*redeem, free*) and LOSE (*forfeit, deplete*). Such distinctions are not captured in the lexical resource, but are algorithmically resolved during ask/framing detection, where contextual clues provide disambiguation capability. For example, *Redeem coupon* is a directive with an implicit request to click a link, i.e., a PERFORM. By contrast, *Avoid losing account access* is a statement of risk, i.e., a LOSE. The focus here is not on the processes necessary for distinguishing between these contextually-determined senses, but on the organizing principles underlying both, in support of application-oriented resource construction.

LCS+ resource for SE adapted from STYLUS: Setting disambiguation aside, resource improvements are still necessary for the SE domain because, due to its size and coverage, STYLUS is likely to predict a large number of both true and false positives during ask/framing detection. To reduce false positives without taking a hit to true positives, we leverage an important property of the LCS paradigm: its extensible organizational structure wherein similar verbs are grouped together. With just one person-day of effort by two computational linguists (authors on the paper; the algorithm developer, also an author, was not involved in this process), a new lexical organization, referred to as "LCS+" is derived from STYLUS, taken together with asks/framings from a set of 46 malicious/legitimate emails.[3] These emails are a random

[2]LCS is publicly available at `https://github.com/ihmc/LCS`.

[3]It should be noted that this resource adaptation is based on an analysis of emails not related to, and without access to, the adjudicated ground truth described in section 3. That is, the 46 emails used for resource adaptation are distinct from the 20 emails used for creating adjudicated ground truth.

subset of 1000+ emails (69 malicious and 938 legitimate) sent from an external red team to five volunteers in a large government agency using social engineering tactics. Verbs from these emails are tied into particular LCS classes with matching semantic peers and argument structures. These emails are proprietary but the resulting lexicon is released here: `https://social-threats.github.io/panacea-ask-detection/resources/lcsPlus_classes_based_verbsList.txt`.
Two categories (PERFORM and LOSE) are modified from the adaptation of LCS+ beyond those in STYLUS:

- PERFORM (6 del, 44 added): copy, notify
- GIVE (no changes)
- LOSE (174 del, 11 added): forget, surrender
- GAIN (no changes)

Table 2 shows the refined lexical organization for LCS+ with ask categories (PERFORM, GIVE) and framing categories (GAIN, LOSE). Boldfaced class numbers indicate the STYLUS classes that were modified. The resulting LCS+ resource drives our SE detection/response system. Each class includes italicized examples with boldfaced triggers. The table details changes to PERFORM and LOSE categories. For PERFORM, there are 6 deleted verbs across 10.2 (Banish Verbs) and 30.2 (Sight Verbs) and also 44 new verbs added to 30.2. For LOSE, 7 classes are associated with additions and/or deletions, as detailed in the table.

Thesaurus baseline: The Thesaurus baseline is based on an expansion of simple forms of framings. Specifically, the verbs *gain*, *lose*, *give*, and *perform*, are used as search terms to find related verbs in a standard but robust resource `thesaurus.com` (referred to as "Thesaurus"). The verbs thus found are grouped into these same four categories:

- PERFORM (44): act, do, execute, perform
- GIVE (55): commit, donate, grant, provide
- LOSE (41): expend, forefeit, expend, squander
- GAIN (53): clean, get, obtain, profit, reap

The resulting Thesaurus verb list is publicly released here: `https://social-threats.github.io/panacea-ask-detection/resources/thesaurus_based_verbsList.txt`.

We also adopt categorial variations through CATVAR (Habash and Dorr, 2003) to map between different parts of speech, e.g., *winner*(N) $\rightarrow$ *win*(V). STYLUS, LCS+ and Thesaurus contain verbs only, but asks/framings are often nominalized. For example, *you can reference your gift card* is an implicit ask to examine a gift card, yet without CATVAR this ask is potentially missed. CATVAR recognizes *reference* as a nominal form of *refer*, thus enabling the identification of this ask as a PERFORM.

3. Experiments and Results

Intrinsic evaluation of our resources is based on comparison of ask/framing detection to an adjudicated ground truth (henceforth, GT), a set of 472 clauses from system output on 20 unseen emails. These 20 emails are a random subset of 2600+ messages collected in an email account set up to receive messages from an internal red team as well as "legitimate" messages from corporate and academic mailing lists. As alluded to earlier, these 20 emails are distinct from the dataset used for resource adaptation to produce the task-related LCS+.
The GT is produced through human adjudication and correction by a computational linguist[4] of initial ask/framing labels automatically assigned by our system to the 472 clauses. System output also includes the identification of a "top ask" for each email, based on the degree to which ask argument positions are filled.[5] *Top asks* are adjudicated by the computational linguist once the ask/framing labels are adjudicated. The resulting GT is accessible here: `https://social-threats.github.io/panacea-ask-detection/data/`.
The GT is used to measure the precision/recall/F of three of three variants of ask detection output (Ask, Framing, and Top Ask) corresponding to our three lexica: Thesaurus, STYLUS, and LCS+. LCS+ is favored (with statistical significance) against the two very strong baselines, Thesaurus and STYLUS. Table 3 presents results: Recall for framings is highest for STYLUS, but at the cost of higher false positives (lower precision). F-scores increase for STYLUS over Thesaurus, and for LCS+ over STYLUS.
McNemar (McNemar, 1947) tests yield statistically significant differences for asks/framings at the 2% level between Thesaurus and LCS+ and between STYLUS and LCS+.[6] It should be noted that not all clauses in GT are ask or framing: vast majority (80%) are neither (i.e., they are true negatives).
We note that an alternative to the Thesaurus and LCS baselines would be a bag-of-words lexicon, with no organizational structure. However, the key contribution of this work is the ease of adaptation through classes, obviating the need for training data (which are exceedingly difficult to obtain). Classes enable extension of a small set of verbs to a larger range of options, e.g., if the human determines from a small set of task-related emails that *provide* is relevant, the task-adapted lexicon will include *administer*, *contribute*, and *donate* for free. If a class-based lexical organization is replaced by bag-of-words, we stand to lose efficient (1-person-day) resource adaptation and, moreover, training data would be needed.
A first step toward *extrinsic* evaluation is inspection of responses generated from each resource's top ask/framing pairs. Table 1 (given earlier) shows LCS+ ask/framing pairs

[4]The adjudicator is an author but is not the algorithm developer, who is also an author.

[5]Argument positions express information such as the ask type (i.e. PERFORM), context to the ask (i.e. financial), and the ask target (e.g., "you" in "Did you send me the money?").

[6]Tested values were TP+TN vs FP+FN, i.e., significance of change in total error rate.

PERFORM:

9.1 Put Verbs: ***Position** your cursor here*
10.1 Remove Verbs: ***Delete** virus from machine*
10.2 Banish Verbs→5 deleted (banish, deport, evacuate, extradite, recall): ***Remove** fee from your account*
10.5 Steal Verbs: ***Redeem** coupon below*
10.6 Cheat Verbs: ***Free** yourself from debt*
11.3 Bring and Take Verbs: ***Bring** me a gift card*
13.5.2 Obtain: ***Purchase** two gift cards*
30.2 Sight Verbs→1 deleted (regard), 44 added (e.g., check, eye, try, view, visit): ***View** this website*
37.1 Transfer of Message: ***Ask** for a refund*
37.2 Tell Verbs: ***Tell** them $50 per card*
37.4 Communication: ***Sign** the back of the card*
42.1 Murder Verbs: ***Eliminate** your debt here*
44 Destroy Verbs: ***Destroy** the card*
54.4 Price Verbs: ***Calculate** an amount here*

GIVE:

11.1 Send Verbs: ***Send** me the gift cards*
13.1 Give Verbs: ***Give** today*
13.2 Contribute Verbs: ***Donate**!*
13.3 Future Having: ***Advance** me $100*
13.4.1 Verbs of Fulfilling: ***Credit** your account*
32.1 Want Verbs: *I **need** three gift cards*

LOSE:

10.5 Steal Verbs→11 added (e.g., forfeit, lose, relinquish, sacrifice): *Don't **forfeit** this chance!*
10.6 Cheat Verbs: *Are your funds **depleted**?*
17.1 Throw Verbs: *Don't **toss** out this coupon*
17.2 Pelt Verbs: *Scams **bombarding** you?*
18.1 Hit Verbs: *Don't be **beaten** by debt*
18.2 Swat Verbs: ***Sluggish** market getting you down?*
18.3 Spank Verbs: ***Clobbered** by fees?*
18.4 Impact by Contact: *Avoid being **hit** by malware*
19 Poke Verbs: ***Stuck** with debt?*
29.2 Characterize Verbs→16 deleted (e.g., appreciate, envisage): ***Repudiated** by creditors?*
29.7 Orphan Verbs→5 deleted (apprentice, canonize, cuckold, knight, recruit): *Avoid **crippling** debt*
29.8 Captain Verbs→35 deleted (e.g., captain, coach, cox, escort): ***Bullied** by bill collectors?*
31.1 Amuse Verbs→91 deleted (e.g., amaze, amuse, gladden): *Don't be **disarmed** by hackers*
31.2 Admire Verbs→26 deleted (e.g., admire, exalt); *Are you **lamenting** your credit score?*
31.3 Marvel Verbs→1 deleted (feel): *Living in **fear**?*
33 Judgment Verbs: *Need to remove **penalties**?*
37.8 Complain Verbs: *Want your **gripes** answered?*
42.1 Murder Verbs: *Debt **killing** your credit?*
42.2 Poison Verbs: ***Strangled** by debt?*
44 Destroy Verbs: *PC **destroyed** by malware?*
48.2 Disappearance: *Your account will **expire***
51.2 Leave Verbs: *Found your **abandoned** prize*

GAIN:

13.5.1 Get: *You are a **winner** of 1M Eu.*
13.5.2 Obtain: *You can **recover** your credit rating*

Table 2: Lexical organization of LCS+ relies on Ask Categories (PERFORM, GIVE) and Framing Categories (GIVE, LOSE). Italicized exemplars with boldfaced triggers illustrate usage for each class. Boldfaced class numbers indicate those STYLUS classes that were modified to yield the LCS+ resource.

Thesaurus	**P**	**R**	**F**
Ask:	0.273	0.042	0.072
Framing:	0.265	0.360	0.305
TopAsk:	0.273	0.057	0.094
STYLUS	**P**	**R**	**F**
Ask:	0.333	0.104	0.159
Framing:	0.298	**0.636**	0.406
TopAsk:	0.571	0.151	0.239
LCS+	**P**	**R**	**F**
Ask:	**0.667**	**0.411**	**0.508**
Framing:	**0.600**	0.600	**0.600**
TopAsk:	**0.692**	**0.340**	**0.456**

Table 3: Impact of lexical resources on ask/framing detection: Thesaurus, STYLUS, LCS+

whose corresponding (T)hesaurus and (S)TYLUS pairs are:

(a) **T**: None, None
  S: None, GAIN/won(1.7Eu)
(b) **T**: PERFORM/do(that), LOSE/lose(money)
  S: GAIN/won(money), GIVE/send(money)
(c) **T**: None, GAIN/get(20%)
  S: PERFORM/sign(http:..), GAIN/get(20%)

Below are corresponding examples of generated responses[7] for all 3 resources, based on a templatic approach that leverages ask/framing hierarchical structure and corresponding confidence scores. This module is part of a larger, separate publication.

(a) **T**: How are you? Thanks.
  S: ...too good to be true. What should I do?
  L+: I will contact asap.
(b) **T**: Thanks for getting in touch, need more info.
  S: Nervous about this. Your name?
  L+: I would respond,[8] but I need more info.
(c) **T**: What should I do now?
  S: Website doesn't open, is this the link?
  L+: Thanks, need more info before I paste link

There are qualitative differences in these responses. For example, in (a) Thesaurus (T) yields no asks/framings; thus a canned response is generated. By contrast, the same email yields a more responsive output for STYLUS (S), and a more focused response for LCS+ (L). Similar distinctions are found for responses in (b) and (c). Note that in the LCS+ condition, if there is no match found using LCS+, downstream response generation prompts the attacker (e.g., "please clarify") until an interpretable ask or framing appears. In this SE task, not all responses move the conversation forward. A central goal of the SE task is to waste the attacker's time, play along, and possibly extract information that could unveil their identity.

4. Related Work

LCS is used in interlingual machine translation (Voss and Dorr, 1995; Habash and Dorr, 2002), lexical acquisition

[7]For brevity, *excerpts* are shown in lieu of full emails.
[8]LCS+ detects both GIVE/send and PERFORM/respond.

(Habash et al., 2006), cross-language information retrieval (Levow et al., 2000), language generation (Traum and Habash, 2000), and intelligent language tutoring (Dorr, 1997). STYLUS (Dorr and Voss, 2018) and (Dorr and Olsen, 2018) systematizes LCS based on several studies (Levin and Rappaport Hovav, 1995; Rappaport Hovav and Levin, 1998), but to our knowledge our work is the first use of LCS in a conversational context, within a cyber domain.

Our approach relates to work on conversational agents (CAs), where neural models automatically generate responses (Gao et al., 2019; Santhanam and Shaikh, 2019), topic models produce focused responses (Dziri et al., 2018), self-disclosure yields targeted responses (Ravichander and Black, 2018), and SE detection employs topic models (Bhakta and Harris, 2015) and NLP of conversations (Sawa et al., 2016). However, all such approaches are limited to a pre-defined set of topics, constrained by the training corpus.

Other prior work focuses on persuasion detection/ prediction (Hidey and McKeown, 2018) by leveraging argument structure, but for the purpose of judging when a persuasive attempt might be successful in subreddit discussions dedicated to changing opinions (ChangeMyView). Our work aims to achieve effective dialogue for countering (rather than adopting) persuasive attempts.

Text-based semantic analysis for SE detection (Kim et al., 2018) is related to our work but differs in that our work focuses not just on *detecting* an attack, but on *engaging* with an attacker. Whereas a bot might be employed to warn a potential victim that an attack is underway, our bots are designed to communicate with a social engineer in ways that elicit identifying information.

5. Conclusions

Both STYLUS and LCS+ support ask/framing detection in service of bot-produced responses. Intrinsically, LCS+ is superior to both STYLUS and Thesaurus when measured against human-adjudicated output, verified for significance by McNemar tests at the 2% level. Extrinsically, STYLUS supports more responsive bot outputs and LCS+ supports more focused bot outputs.

A more general advantage of adapting LCS+ to the SE domain is that it can act as a guideline for developing similar resources for other domains which will similarly support focused outputs appropriate for particular domains. The main contribution of this paper is not development of a particular task-specific resource, nor to suggest that LCS+ is a generic resource for many tasks, but to present a systematic, efficient approach to resource adaptation technique that can generalize to other tasks for improved task-specific performance, e.g., understanding viewpoints in social media or detecting motives behind activities of political groups. We acknowledge that our extrinsic evaluation is limited. While we have demonstrated the efficacy of ask detection approaches on a set of representative emails, a quantitative evaluation is required to test the statistical significance of our extrinsic observations. Future work is planned to conduct experiments with crowd-sourced workers judging the efficacy and effectiveness of generated responses.

Acknowledgments

This work was supported by DARPA through AFRL Contract FA8650-18- C-7881 and through Army Contract W31P4Q-17-C-0066. All statements of fact, opinion or conclusions contained herein are those of the authors and should not be construed as representing the official views or policies of DARPA, AFRL, Army, or the U.S. Government.

6. Bibliographical References

Bhakta, R. and Harris, I. G. (2015). Semantic analysis of dialogs to detect social engineering attacks. *Proceedings of the 2015 IEEE 9th International Conference on Semantic Computing (IEEE ICSC 2015)*, pages 424–427.

Chang, S. C., Shahani, R. C., Cipollone, D. J., Calcagno, M. V., Olsen, M. J. B., and Parkinson, D. J. (2007). Linguistic Object Model, January. 7,171,352.

Chang, S. C., Shahani, R. C., Cipollone, D. J., Calcagno, M. V., Olsen, M. J. B., and Parkinson, D. J. (2010). Lexical Semantic Structure, March. 7,689,410.

Dorr, B. J. and Olsen, M. B. (2018). Lexical conceptual structure of literal and metaphorical spatial language: A case study of push. In *Proceedings of the First International Workshop on Spatial Language Understanding*, pages 31–40.

Dorr, B., Bhatia, A., Dalton, A., Mather, B., Hebenstreit, B., Santhanam, S., Cheng, Z., Zemel, S., and Strzalkowski, T. (2020). Detecting asks in social engineering attacks: Impact of linguistic and structural knowledge. In *Proceedings of Thirty-Fourth AAAI Conference on Artificial Intelligence 2020.*

Dorr, B. J. (1993). *Machine Translation: A View from the Lexicon*. MIT Press, Cambridge, MA.

Dorr, B. J. (1997). Large-Scale Dictionary Construction for Foreign Language Tutoring and Interlingual Machine Translation. *Machine Translation*, 12:271–322.

Drew, P. and Couper-Kuhlen, E. (2014). *Requesting in social interaction*. John Benjamins Publishing Company.

Dziri, N., Kamalloo, E., Mathewson, K. W., and Zaiane, O. (2018). Augmenting neural response generation with context-aware topical attention. *arXiv preprint arXiv:1811.01063*.

Gao, J., Galley, M., Li, L., et al. (2019). Neural approaches to conversational ai. *Foundations and Trends® in Information Retrieval*, 13(2-3):127–298.

Habash, N. and Dorr, B. J. (2002). Handling Translation Divergences: Combining Statistical and Symbolic Techniques in Generation-Heavy Machine Translation. In *Proceedings of the Fifth Conference of the Association for Machine Translation in the Americas*, pages 84–93, Tiburon, CA.

Habash, N., Dorr, B. J., and Monz, C. (2006). Challenges in Building an Arabic GHMT system with SMT Components. In *Proceedings of the 7th Conference of the Association for Machine Translation in the Americas*, pages 56–65, Boston, MA, August.

Hidey, C. and McKeown, K. (2018). Persuasive Influence Detection: The Role of Argument Sequencing. In *Proceedings of the Thirty-Second AAAI Conference on Arti-*

ficial Intelligence, pages 5173–5180, San Francisco, California, USA.

Jackendoff, R. (1983). *Semantics and Cognition*. MIT Press, Cambridge, MA.

Jackendoff, R. (1990). *Semantic Structures*. MIT Press, Cambridge, MA.

Jackendoff, R. (1996). The Proper Treatment of Measuring Out, Telicity, and Perhaps Even Quantification in English. *Natural Language and Linguistic Theory*, 14:305–354.

Kim, M., Song, C., Kim, H., Park, D., Kwon, Y., Namkung, E., Harris, I. G., and Carlsson, M. (2018). Catch me, yes we can!-pwning social engineers using natural language processing techniques in real-time.

Kipper, K., Korhonen, A., Ryant, N., and Palmer, M. (2007). A Large-scale Classification of English Verbs. In *Language Resources and Evaluation*.

Levin, B. and Rappaport Hovav, M. (1995). *Unaccusativity: At the Syntax-Lexical Semantics Interface, Linguistic Inquiry Monograph 26*. MIT Press, Cambridge, MA.

Levin, B. (1993). *English Verb Classes and Alternations: A Preliminary Investigation*. The University of Chicago Press.

Levow, G., Dorr, B. J., and Lin, D. (2000). Construction of Chinese-English Semantic Hierarchy for Cross-language Retrieval.

Rappaport Hovav, M. and Levin, B. (1998). Building Verb Meanings. In M. Butt et al., editors, *The Projection of Arguments: Lexical and Compositional Factors*, pages 97–134. CSLI Publications, Stanford, CA.

McNemar, Q. (1947). Note on the sampling error of the difference between correlated proportions or percentages. *Psychometrika*, 12(2):153–157, jun.

Olsen, M. B. (1994). The Semantics and Pragmatics of Lexical and Grammatical Aspect. *Studies in the Linguistic Sciences*, 24(1–2):361–375.

Palmer, M., Bonial, C., and Hwang, J. D. (2017). VerbNet: Capturing English Verb behavior, Meaning and Usage.

Ravichander, A. and Black, A. W. (2018). An empirical study of self-disclosure in spoken dialogue systems. In *Proceedings of the 19th Annual SIGdial Meeting on Discourse and Dialogue, Melbourne, Australia, July 12-14, 2018*, pages 253–263.

Santhanam, S. and Shaikh, S. (2019). A survey of natural language generation techniques with a focus on dialogue systems-past, present and future directions. *arXiv preprint arXiv:1906.00500*.

Sawa, Y., Bhakta, R., Harris, I., and Hadnagy, C. (2016). Detection of social engineering attacks through natural language processing of conversations. In *Proceedings of the 2016 IEEE Tenth International Conference on Semantic Computing (ICSC)*, pages 262–265, 02.

Traum, D. and Habash, N. (2000). Generation from Lexical Conceptual Structures. In *Proceedings of the Workshop on Applied Interlinguas, North American Association for Computational Linguistics / Applied NLP Conference*, pages 34–41.

Voss, C. R. and Dorr, B. J. (1995). Toward a Lexicalized Grammar for Interlinguas. *J. of Machine Translation*, 10:143–184.

Zemel, A. (2017). Texts as actions: Requests in online chats between reference librarians and library patrons. *Journal of the Association for Information Science and Technology*, 67(7):1687–1697.

7. Language Resource References

Dorr, Bonnie and Voss, Clare. (2018). *STYLUS: A Resource for Systematically Derived Language Usage*. Association for Computational Linguistics.

Nizar Habash and Bonnie J. Dorr. (2003). *A Categorial Variation Database for English*.

Proceedings of the Workshop on Social Threats in Online Conversations: Understanding and Management (STOC-2020), pages 15–20
Language Resources and Evaluation Conference (LREC 2020), Marseille, 11–16 May 2020

Analysis of Online Conversations to Detect Cyberpredators Using Recurrent Neural Networks

Jinhwa Kim, Yoon Jo Kim, Mitra Behzadi, Ian G. Harris
Dankook University, Seoul Women's University, University of California Irvine
Yongin South Korea, Seoul South Korea, Irvine CA USA
best08618@gmail.com, yoonjokim12@gmail.com, mbehzadi@uci.edu, harris@ics.uci.edu

Abstract

We present an automated approach to analyze the text of an online conversation and determine whether one of the participants is a cyberpredator who is preying on another participant. The task is divided into two stages, 1) the classification of each message, and 2) the classification of the entire conversation. Each stage uses a Recurrent Neural Network (RNN) to perform the classification task.

Keywords: Cyberpredator detection, natural language understanding, recurrent neural networks

1. Introduction

Online cyberpredators are a serious threat against children who increasingly use social networking and messaging services to interact with strangers.Our study also found that one in nine teens will received unwanted online solicitations (Madigan et al., 2018). Parents are advised to monitor their children's use of social media, but this is extremely difficult in practice given the variety of networking services and access methods that a child can choose from. Several software tools are available to observe children's online behavior (FlexiSPY, 2019; Easemon Inc., 2019; Cocospy, 2019). However, existing products are limited to recording data for later examination, or providing a "keyword alert" when a particular word has been used in text. These tools do not attempt to understand the semantics of the conversation, so the majority of the burden of identifying cyberpredators is left to the parent's manual effort. Automated approaches which employ natural language understanding could be of tremendous benefit. We present an approach to automatically monitor communications with a child in order to determine if a communication partner is a cyberpredator.

Machine learning approaches, specifically artificial neural networks (ANNs), are generally well suited to this type of classification problem because they can theoretically approximate continuous functions, given a few assumptions. An ANN could be used to classify a conversation as either predatory or non-predatory, however there are several practical difficulties in the application of ANNs to this problem. One issue is the importance of context in understanding the meaning of a conversation. Attempting to infer the intent of a conversation by examining utterances individually will generally produce poor results because sentences in dialogs are meant to be understood in the context of all messages in the dialog. The dependence on extended context requires that the input to the classification process must be a large block of utterances which must be classified as a whole. Another difficulty is the high dimensionality of the input space of the problem, which must capture entire conversations with hundreds of messages.

We address the high dimensionality by dividing the problem into two stages. The first stage classifies the intent of individual messages, and the second stage uses the results of the first stage to classify the entire conversation. The first stage generates a concise summary of the individual messages, allowing the second stage to efficiently consider the meaning of the entire conversation. We address the context in two ways. When classifying individual messages, the first stage also considers the a window of 5 messages which comprise local context. When classifying the entire conversation, the second stage considers the classifications of all messages uttered by the potential attacker in the conversation.

2. Related Work

Much of the existing research in detection of cyberpredators is based on the chat log transcripts provided by Perverted Justice (Perverted Justice Foundation, 2019), a community of volunteers who posed as children in chat rooms in order to lure predators. The efforts of the Perverted Justice community has been credited with resulting in the conviction of 623 cyber-predators to date. Chats with predators have been transcribed and made available to the public. The linguistic properties of the Perverted Justice dataset have been explored in several studies (Black et al., 2015; Chiu et al., 2018). The International Competition for Sexual Predator Identification was held and the PAN 2012 workshop (Inches and Crestani, 2012b), catalyzing interest in the problem. To support the competition, the PAN 2012 dataset was created using the Perverted Justice dataset and enhancing it with adult-to-adult sexual conversations from a repository of Omegle conversations and a set of IRC chat logs (Inches and Crestani, 2012c).

Almost all existing approaches use machine learning approaches to detect predatory text. Many machine learning techniques have been used including Support Vector Machines (Pendar, 2007; Morris and Hirst, 2012; Parapar et al., 2012; Peersman et al., 2012; Villatoro-Tello et al., 2012; Escalante et al., 2013; Vartapetiance and Gillam, 2014; Cheong et al., 2015), Decision Trees (McGhee et al., 2011a; Miah et al., 2011; Kontostathis et al., 2012; Vartapetiance and Gillam, 2014; Cheong et al., 2015), Naive Bayes (Miah et al., 2011; Bogdanova et al., 2012; Vartapetiance and Gillam, 2014; Cheong et al., 2015), k-Nearest Neighbor

(Pendar, 2007; Cheong et al., 2015), logistic regression (Miah et al., 2011; Cheong et al., 2015), Maximum Entropy (Eriksson and Karlgren, 2012), and Multilayer Perceptron (MLP) Neural Networks (Villatoro-Tello et al., 2012; Escalante et al., 2013; Cheong et al., 2015). A rule-based heuristic was presented (McGhee et al., 2011a; Kontostathis et al., 2012) and shown to outperform a decision tree approach.

All approaches, other than those based on Neural Networks, require the explicit definition of set of features used to represent the conversation. All of these approaches have used lexical features, unigrams and bigrams which are associated with speech acts commonly performed by attackers. Words are grouped into dictionaries which are assumed to indicate the conversational goals of a predator. Examples of lexical features include the number of desensitization verbs (e.g. kiss, suck) and the number of reframing verbs (e.g. teach, practice) (McGhee et al., 2011a; Kontostathis et al., 2012). Several approaches use Linguistic Inquiry and Word Count (LIWC) (Pennebaker et al., 2011) features which associate words with cognitive and emotional states. Some approaches use conversational/behavioral features which model properties of the overall dialog such as the number of conversation participants, the length of the conversation (Eriksson and Karlgren, 2012), the number of initiations, and the number of questions (Morris and Hirst, 2012).

Several previous approaches have employed MLP neural networks to identify predators (Villatoro-Tello et al., 2012; Escalante et al., 2013; Cheong et al., 2015). Neural networks do not require an explicit set of features. Instead, these previous approaches use a bag-of-words representation which summarizes a conversation as the number of occurrences of each word in the vocabulary, regardless of sequence.

3. Cyberpredator Intent Classification

Early work in the study of online child exploitation presented a set of conversational goals of predators and categorized the utterances of a predator based on the goal being achieved. A typology is presented by O'Connell (O'Connell, 2003) which describes 5 stages on conversation: friendship forming, relationship forming, risk assessment, exclusivity, and sexual. An alternate classification is presented by Olson (Olson et al., 2007) which contains 3 main classes: grooming, isolation, and approach.

Researchers in (McGhee et al., 2011a) present a classification of cyberpredator intents and a tool, ChatCoder2, which uses a rule-based approach to classify messages according to their classification. We use the classification presented in (McGhee et al., 2011a) because it has been shown to be effective, and because we can use the ChatCoder2 tool to generate a labeled dataset which we use for training. Each message is placed in one of the following 4 classes.

- **Exchange of personal information (200)** - This includes questions about semi-personal information which might be exchanged between new friends. Topics include age, gender, location, boyfriends/girlfriends, and likes/dislikes. The cyberpredator uses this to initiate a trust relationship.
- **Grooming (600)** - This involves the use of sexual terminology, regardless of context. Cyberpredators often use this to desensitize the victim to sexual discussions.
- **Approach (900)** - This describes when the cyberpredator is either gathering information to arrange a meeting, or encouraging the victim to keep their relationship secret.
- **Non-predatory (000)** - These are all messages not in one of the previous classes.

4. System Architecture

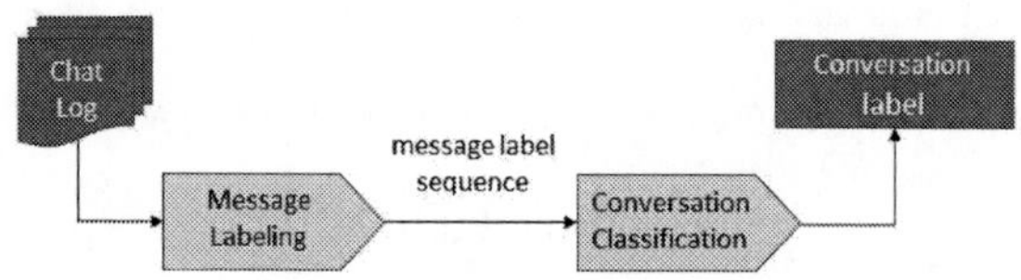

Figure 1: Overall Structure

The overall structure of our approach is illustrated in Figure 1. Our approach is divided into two stages. The first stage is *Message Labeling* which labels each of the message from the potential attacker with its intent classification. The second stage is *Conversation Classification* which evaluates the entire sequence of messages from the potential attacker and determines if the potential attacker is a predator or not. The input to the Conversation Classification stage is not a sequence of messages. Instead, it is the sequence of sentence labels produced by the Message Labeling stage.

Message Labeling During the Message Labeling stage, each message from the potential attacker in a dialogue is categorized by its intent classification. For categorizing each message, we train the mapping pattern between a message and the categories. Because the messages are written in natural language, each message must be converted in to the form of a vector to be used by the training model. In order to capture the meaning of each message, we must consider not only the words in the message and their sequence, but also the preceding messages which comprise the context in the conversation. We use two different methods to represent the meaning of a message, one method to represent meaning in a single message, and a second method to consider the impact of context.

We generate message encodings using the Universal Sentence Encoder (Cer et al., 2018a) approach to generate a message vector. This is in contrast to other traditional methods such as word2vec embeddings (Mikolov et al., 2013) or bag-of-words model. Word embeddings have been shown to perform well at capturing the meaning of individual words. However, the bag-of-words model loses meaning information because it ignores the ordering of words in the message. The Universal Sentence Encoding approach uses an LSTM (Long Short-Term Memory models) model to understand the relationship between each word. For this reason, Universal Sentence Encoding is more suitable and we employ it using its TensorFlow (Cer et al., 2018b) implementation.

In addition, the meaning of a message is determined in part by the context which precedes it. Though two statements look similar, they could have different meanings depends on their preceding contexts. The message “Call me” could be a message from the two close friends while it could be one that a predator leads a victim to call him or her. In this case, it is hard to identify where it would belong to with only one message. For this reason, when classifying a message, we consider the 4 messages preceding the message in question. So classification is performed by examining a window of 5 messages in order to consider conversational context.

Figure 2 is the structure of our training model for Message Labeling. The window of 5 messages, ending with the message being classified, are input to a layer which uses Universal Sentence Encoding to generate a 1*512 dimension vector for each message. The vectors from the encoding layer become the input of the succeeding LSTM and then Dense layer. By considering the window of 5 vectors at the LSTM/Dense layers, our approach can infer local context.

Conversation Classification After labeling each message, each conversation is represented as a sequence of labeled statements. These label values are used as the value of the vector for input to the *Conversation Classification* stage. Figure 3 shows the structure of our model of the Conversation Classification stage. The sequence of message labels is padded to ensure that the length of the input vector is constant. However, the padded labels must not be considered as the labels of the conversation. Therefore, we use the Masking layer, which is used to ignore padded labels. We use an LSTM layer to train the corresponding pattern of labels and then a Dense layer for final classification of the conversation.

5. Experiments

We present two sets of results. The first set of results evaluate the Message Labeling stage alone by presenting the precision and recall of the message labeling process. The second set of results evaluates both the Message Labeling and Conversation Classification stages together by presenting the precision and recall of the classification of a set of conversations.

5.1. Dataset

To evaluate the Message Labeling stage, we use chatlog data from both ChatCoder2 (McGhee et al., 2011b) and PAN2012 (Inches and Crestani, 2012a). ChatCoder2 provides conversations extracted from the Perverted-Justice (PJ) website (Perverted Justice Foundation, 2019). All of the conversations in the ChatCoder2 dataset are predatory, while the PAN2012 dataset if a mix of predatory and non-predatory conversations. ChatCoder2 is an heuristic tool which automatically labels each message with its intent classification (’000’, ’200’, ’600’, and ’900’). We use ChatCoder2 to automatically classify the messages in each conversation.

Table 1 describes the set of messages used to evaluate the Message Labeling stage. A total of 5008 messages are used and are taken from both the ChatCoder2 and PAN2012 datasets. Our goal was to use the same number of messages in each predatory intent (’200’, ’600’, and ’900’), so we extracted 626 of each type of message from the ChatCoder2 dataset, and we selected another 626 messages with non-predatory intents (’000’) from the ChatCoder2 dataset for balance. The number 626 was chosen because that is the largest number of messages that we could select while maintaining balance in each intent. In other words, 626 is the minimum of the number of messages in each class in the ChatCoder2 dataset. In total, 2504 (626 * 4) messages are selected from the ChatCoder2 dataset. We expect that using non-predatory messages (’000’) only from the ChatCoder2 dataset would result in a biased classification because all of the non-predatory sentences would be taken from predatory conversations. For this reason, we selected another 2504 non-predatory messages from the PAN2012 dataset as well.

Total Dataset	Number
♯ of Conversations	119
♯ of Total Messages	5008
♯ of Messages in Category ‘000’	3130
♯ of Messages in Category ’200’	626
♯ of Messages in Category ’600’	626
♯ of Messages in Category ’900’	626

Table 1: Dataset used to evaluate Message Labeling

Total Dataset	Number
♯ of Conversations	480
♯ of Predatory Conversations	128
♯ of Non-Predatory Conversations	352
♯ of Total Messages	78130

Table 2: Dataset used to evaluate Conversation Classification

To evaluate the Conversation Classification stage, we use only the PAN2012 dataset for training and test. We use only conversations with more than 130 messages. The sequence of labeled messages from the output of Message Labeling are used as input for Conversation Classification. Conversations in the PAN2012 dataset are pre-labeled as predatory and non-predatory. Table 2 describes the properties of the dataset to evaluate Conversation Classification.

5.2. Results of Message Labeling

For training the network used for Message Labeling, we use 10 epochs use a batch size of 32. We use 80% of the dataset for training and 20% for testing. Table 3 shows the precision and recall values for each label, independently. Both training and testing are performed on an Intel Xeon CPU,

	Label	000	200	600	900
Training	Precision	0.93	0.76	0.73	0.68
	Recall	0.91	0.78	0.79	0.65
Test	Precision	0.91	0.77	0.73	0.68
	Recall	0.92	0.78	0.79	0.64

Table 3: Performance results of Message Labeling

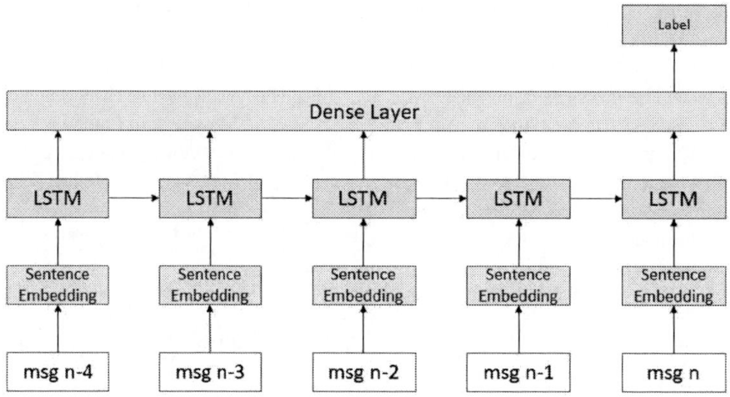

Figure 2: Structure of *Message Labeling*

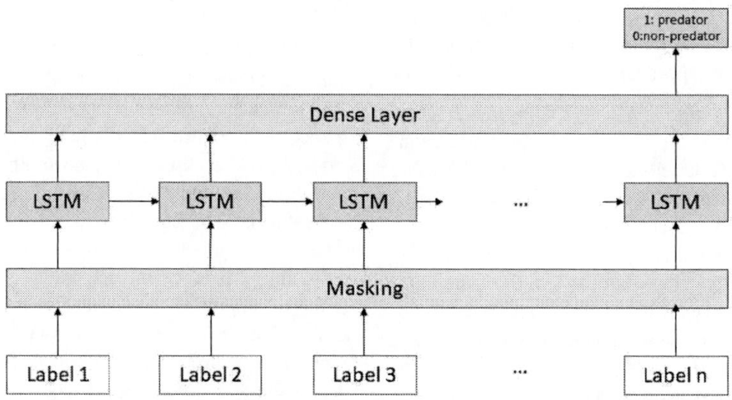

Figure 3: Structure of *Conversation Classification*

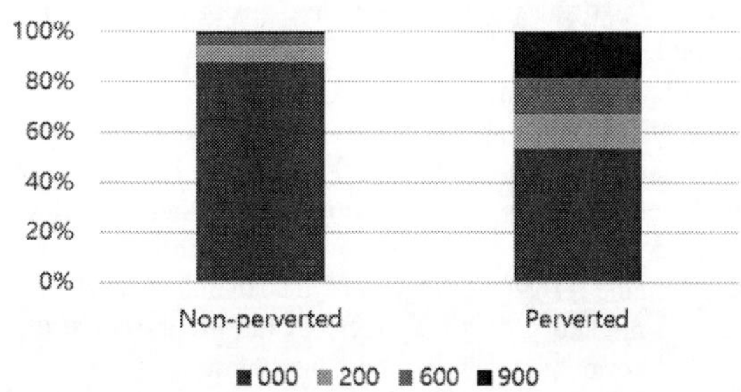

Figure 4: Distributions of each label in conversations from either predator or non-predator

2.3GHz clock rate, with a Tesla K80 GPU, within Google Colaboratory. The entire training process is performed in 1 minute and 12 seconds. Sentence embedding requires 29 seconds of the total time.

5.3. Results of Conversation Classification

Conversation Classification was evaluated by using Message Labeling to label each message in the PAN2012 dataset, and using the resulting message label sequences to classify each conversation. Table 4 shows the number of sentences with each label in the PAN 2012 dataset, as derived using the trained model for Message Labeling. Figure 4 shows the distribution of different message labels in both predatory and non-predatory conversations. In non-predatory conversations, the vast majority of messages, 88%, are classified in set '000' as clearly non-malicious. In predatory conversations, the percentage of '000' messages is lower, 53%, and the other potentially predatory message classes are much more common.

Label	000	200	600	900
♯ of messages	59142	7060	6262	5666

Table 4: Number of PAN 2012 messages in each class

Predicted	Actual	
	Predatory	Non-predatory
Predatory	29(TP)	3(FP)
Non-predatory	2(FN)	62(TN)

Table 5: Performance results of categorization conversations

When training the model for Conversation Classification, we set the maximum length of the sequence as 200 and the input whose length is lower than 200 is padded. We use 10 epochs and set batch size to 32. We use 80%(384) of the dataset for training and 20%(96) for the test. Our model yields precision of *0.9063*, recall of *0.9355*, F1 score of *0.9148*, and F0.5 score of *0.9058*. Table 5 shows the detail of the performance results. We compare our results to those presented at the PAN2012 cyberpredator detection competition (Inches and Crestani, 2012b), although our dataset included ChatCoder2 data, in addition to the PAN2012 data used in the competition. Compared to the 16 competitors used for official evaluation, our results place us first with respect to recall, first with respect to F1 score, third with respect to F0.5 score, and fifth with respect to precision. We argue that recall is the most important measure for this problem because it indicates the fraction of predators who would go undetected. We expect that a parent would be more willing to accept a small number of false alarms rather than risking the possibility of missing a predator.

6. Conclusions

We have presented an approach to the detection of predatory conversations which first classifies individual messages and uses those results to classify entire conversations. RNNs are used to perform each stage and are trained using messages labeled by the ChatCoder2 tool and existing prelabeled conversations. Limited context is considered in the labeling of individual messages by considering the previous 4 messages when classifying a message. Our approach provides better recall than previous approaches.

7. Ethical Considerations

Our contribution is focused on helping to protect children from cyberpredators. We do not foresee any malicious use of this technology.

8. Acknowledgements

This material is based upon work supported by the National Science Foundation under Grant No. 1813858. This research was also supported by a generous gift from the Herman P. & Sophia Taubman Foundation.

9. Bibliographical References

Black, P. J., Wollis, M. A., Woodworth, M., and Hancock, J. T. (2015). A linguistic analysis of grooming strategies of online child sex offenders: Implications for our understanding of predatory sexual behavior in an increasingly computer-mediated world. *Child abuse & neglect*, 44.

Bogdanova, D., Rosso, P., and Solorio, T. (2012). On the impact of sentiment and emotion based features in detecting online sexual predators. In *Proceedings of the 3rd Workshop in Computational Approaches to Subjectivity and Sentiment Analysis*, WASSA '12.

Cer, D., Yang, Y., Kong, S., Hua, N., Limtiaco, N., John, R. S., Constant, N., Guajardo-Cespedes, M., Yuan, S., Tar, C., Sung, Y., Strope, B., and Kurzweil, R. (2018a). Universal sentence encoder. *CoRR*, abs/1803.11175.

Cer, D., Yang, Y., yi Kong, S., Hua, N., Limtiaco, N., St. John, R., Constant, N., Guajardo-Céspedes, M., Yuan, S., Tar, C., Sung, Y. H., Strope, B., and Kurzweil, R. (2018b). Universal sentence encoder for English. *EMNLP 2018 - Conference on Empirical Methods in Natural Language Processing: System Demonstrations, Proceedings*, pages 169–174.

Cheong, Y., Jensen, A. K., Guonadottir, E. R., Bae, B., and Togelius, J. (2015). Detecting predatory behavior in game chats. *IEEE Transactions on Computational Intelligence and AI in Games*, 7(3), Sep.

Chiu, M. M., Seigfried-Spellar, K. C., and Ringenberg, T. R. (2018). Exploring detection of contact vs. fantasy online sexual offenders in chats with minors: Statistical discourse analysis of self-disclosure and emotion words. *Child abuse & neglect*, 81.

Cocospy. (2019). Cocospy. https://www.cocospy.com.

Easemon Inc. (2019). iKeyMonitor. https://ikeymonitor.com.

Eriksson, G. and Karlgren, J. (2012). Features for modelling characteristics of conversations: Notebook for pan at clef 2012. In *CLEF (Online Working Notes/Labs/Workshop)*.

Escalante, H. J., Villatoro-Tello, E., Juárez, A., Montes-y Gómez, M., and Villaseñor, L. (2013). Sexual predator detection in chats with chained classifiers. In *Proceedings of the 4th Workshop on Computational Approaches to Subjectivity, Sentiment and Social Media Analysis*, June.

FlexiSPY. (2019). FlexiSPY. https://www.flexispy.com.

Inches, G. and Crestani, F. (2012a). Overview of the International Sexual Predator Identification Competitin at PAN-2012. *Working Notes Papers of the CLEF 2012 Evaluation Labs*, (May).

Inches, G. and Crestani, F. (2012b). Overview of the international sexual predator identification competition at pan-2012. In *CLEF (Online Working Notes/Labs/Workshop)*.

Inches, G. and Crestani, F. (2012c). Overview of the international sexual predator identification competition at pan-2012. In *CLEF*.

Kontostathis, A., Garron, A., Reynolds, K., West, W., and Edwards, L. (2012). Identifying predators using chatcoder 2.0. In *CLEF (Online Working Notes/Labs/Workshop)*.

Madigan, S., Villani, V., Azzopardi, C., Laut, D., Smith, T., Temple, J. R., Browne, D., and Dimitropoulos, G. (2018). The prevalence of unwanted online sexual exposure and solicitation among youth: A meta-analysis. *Journal of Adolescent Health*, 63(2):133 – 141.

McGhee, I., Bayzick, J., Kontostathis, A., Edwards, L., McBride, A., and Jakubowski, E. (2011a). Learning to identify internet sexual predation. *International Journal of Electronic Commerce*, 15(3):103–122.

McGhee, I., Bayzick, J., Kontostathis, A., Edwards, L., McBride, A., and Jakubowski, E. (2011b). Learning to identify Internet sexual predation. *International Journal of Electronic Commerce*, 15(3):103–122.

Miah, M. W. R., Yearwood, J., and Kulkarni, S. (2011). Detection of child exploiting chats from a mixed chat dataset as a text classification task. In *Proceedings of the Australasian Language Technology Association Workshop 2011*, December.

Mikolov, T., Yih, W. T., and Zweig, G. (2013). Linguistic regularities in continuous spaceword representations. *NAACL HLT 2013 - 2013 Conference of the North American Chapter of the Association for Computational Linguistics: Human Language Technologies, Proceedings of the Main Conference*, pages 746–751.

Morris, C. and Hirst, G. (2012). Identifying sexual predators by svm classification with lexical and behavioral features. In *CLEF (Online Working Notes/Labs/Workshop)*.

Olson, L. N., Daggs, J. L., Ellevold, B. L., and Rogers, T. K. K. (2007). Entrapping the innocent: Toward a theory of child sexual predators' luring communication. *Communication Theory*, 17(3).

O'Connell, R. L. (2003). A typology of child cybersexploitation and online grooming practices. Preston: University of Central Lancashire, Cybersex Research Unit.

Parapar, J., Losada, D. E., and Barreiro, A. (2012). A learning-based approach for the identification of sexual predators in chat logs. In *CLEF (Online Working Notes/Labs/Workshop)*.

Peersman, C., Vaassen, F., Van Asch, V., and Daelemans, W. (2012). Conversation level constraints on pedophile detection in chat rooms. In *CLEF (Online Working Notes/Labs/Workshop)*.

Pendar, N. (2007). Toward spotting the pedophile telling victim from predator in text chats. In *International Conference on Semantic Computing (ICSC 2007)*, Sep.

Pennebaker, J. W., Chung, C. K., Ireland, M. E., Gonzales, A. L., and Booth, R. J. (2011). The development and psychometric properties of liwc2007.

Perverted Justice Foundation. (2019). Perverted Justice. `www.perverted-justice.com`. Accessed: 2019-11-08.

Vartapetiance, A. and Gillam, L. (2014). "our little secret": pinpointing potential predators. *Security Informatics*, 3(1):3, Sep.

Villatoro-Tello, E., Juárez-González, A., Escalante, H. J., y Gómez, M. M., and Pineda, L. V. (2012). A two-step approach for effective detection of misbehaving users in chats. In *CLEF (Online Working Notes/Labs/Workshop)*.

Proceedings of the Workshop on Social Threats in Online Conversations: Understanding and Management (STOC-2020), pages 21–28
Language Resources and Evaluation Conference (LREC 2020), Marseille, 11–16 May 2020

A Privacy Preserving Data Publishing Middleware for Unstructured, Textual Social Media Data

Prasadi Abeywardana, Uthayasanker Thayasivam
Department of Computer Science and Engineering
University of Moratuwa, Sri Lanka
prasadiapsara.18@cse.mrt.ac.lk, rtuthaya@cse.mrt.ac.lk

Abstract

Privacy is going to be an integral part of data science and analytics in the coming years. The next hype of data experimentation is going to be heavily dependent on privacy preserving techniques mainly as it's going to be a legal responsibility rather than a mere social responsibility. Privacy preservation becomes more challenging specially in the context of unstructured data. Social networks have become predominantly popular over the past couple of decades and they are creating a huge data lake at a high velocity. Social media profiles contain a wealth of personal and sensitive information, creating enormous opportunities for third parties to analyze them with different algorithms, draw conclusions and use in disinformation campaigns and micro targeting based dark advertising. This study provides a mitigation mechanism for disinformation campaigns that are done based on the insights extracted from personal/sensitive data analysis. Specifically, this research is aimed at building a privacy preserving data publishing middleware for unstructured social media data without compromising the true analytical value of those data. A novel way is proposed to apply traditional structured privacy preserving techniques on unstructured data. Creating a comprehensive twitter corpus annotated with privacy attributes is another objective of this research, especially because the research community is lacking one.

Keywords: Privacy Preserving Data Mining, Privacy Preserving Data Publishing, Disinformation, Micro-targeting, Anonymization, Data Utility, Social Networks, Data Science

1. Introduction

Big data being a buzz word which has created an immense hype in the society, many analytical models are employed in order to repurpose those data and derive insights. With the advancements of distributed systems and theoretically cheap storage, there are less constraints to capture data as much as possible and store them. Collection of data related to individuals in a global scale has become mainstream because of this.

Data are collected in big scales and published to be used by different parties for different purposes. At this point of publishing, there should be a proper insurance for personal data, as the publishing party cannot guarantee for which purposes this personal information will be used by the utilizing party.

Micro-targeting based on the third-party analysis done on personal data is used as a means of disinformation campaigns. A famous example for this is dark advertisements targeting specific users in a very personalized manner for sharing misinformation in political campaigns. This is achieved by identifying target users by analyzing their political preferences and showing them personalized dark ads with content they are highly likely to believe. Analyzing sensitive personal information and using them for various intentions without user consents makes it a combination of an ethical and legal concern (Alaphilippe et al., 2019).

1.1 Data Protection Regulations

Until recently, privacy was just a social responsibility, but it's no more like that, because many legal systems have begun to enforce laws on protecting individuals' privacy. Specially incidents like what happened between Facebook and Cambridge Analytica have forced the governments and policy makers to look at personal information protection as an emerging concern. Following are some of such novel legal requirements which arouse recently.

1.1.1 General Data Protection Regulation (GDPR)

This is a regulation imposed by European Union (EU) on data protection and privacy for all individuals within the EU and the European Economic Area (EEA) (Wikipedia, 2016). This is applicable to exporting and processing personal data in a region outside EU as well. The intention of this regulation is to make it easy for non-European companies to work with European bodies without any data breaches.

1.1.2 Russian Federal Law on Personal Data

This is a regulation which emphasizes on systemizing the data processing of individuals in Russia. This emphasizes on localizing personal data of Russian citizens to Russia (KPMG, 2018).

1.1.3 German Bundesdatenschutzgesetz (BDSG)

This governs the exposure of personal data, which are manually processed or stored in IT systems. This was being modified with certain amendments for a long period of time and has become stricter in the recent past.

1.2 Social Threats of Personal Data Analysis

Personal data are coming into analytical systems through various domains. Mobile data, health care data, social media data and web usage data are a few such domains which can pump a huge amount of personal data into analytical systems without the knowledge or consent of individuals. There's one prominent area, which has reformed the sharing of personal information, that is none other than social media. People choose to share many information about themselves as well as their close ones, compromising the privacy of both parties (Mehta and Rao, 2015).

Social platforms offer their data to third parties and advertisers to use in their analysis and campaigns. But sometimes these data are used in micro targeted disinformation campaigns to share dark ads. These highly personalized adverts are heavily used in political contexts to influence voters by sharing misinformation. In order to host micro targeted ad campaigns, a lot of information related to individuals, their preferences and personality are required, and social media undoubtedly contain a fortune of such data. In the recent incident that involved Facebook, Cambridge Analytica and Global Science Research (GSR), millions of US Facebook users' data were analyzed without their consent and used in voter targeting, which is unethical as it sounds (Alaphilippe et al., 2019). A solution to these concerns might be a law enforced privacy preserving middleware that has to be adopted by any social media platform, before publishing their data to a third party.

The purpose of this research is to come up with a framework to sanitize data and preserve privacy, which can be utilized before publishing textual social media data to any analytical 3rd party. This will ensure that any sensitive personal data will not be used in a way where a person's identity is revealed, and the individuals will not be subjected to disinformation campaigns. Specifically, this research addresses the problem of sanitizing social media data, which becomes more challenging due to their unstructured nature. Twitter is used as the selected social media platform to train and evaluate the capabilities of this framework. A corpus of 3000 tweets is built and annotated to be used in the model training process.

The rest of the paper is organized as follows. Some theoretical concepts related to privacy preserving data publishing particularly in the context of unstructured data will be discussed in the background section. Then the methodology adapted will be described followed by a section dedicated towards the dataset. Next section is about the experimental design and the results and after that a section is contributed for discussion and future work. Finally, the paper is concluded with a conclusion section.

2. Background

Publishing sensitive data related to individuals in a way that protects their privacy was a topic of interest for some time and many techniques are implemented with the contribution from various fields such as computer science, statistics and social science. A few theorical concepts from the PPDP domain are described under this section.

2.1 Different Types of Attributes Related to Personal Data

Attributes related to personal data can be classified as follows based on how they can identify an individual. These attributes are extracted and used in PPDP techniques (Mehta and Rao, 2015).

2.1.1 Personal Information Identifiers

These are the attributes such as ID, name or email address that can be directly used to identify an individual. These attributes uniquely recognize individuals from others.

2.1.2 Quasi Identifiers

These are the attributes that can be combined with other external data and used to identify an individual. For instance, age, gender, profession, race, religion can be considered as quasi identifiers. These are not unique identifiers by themselves but can be combined with another set of quasi identifiers to uniquely recognize a person.

2.1.3 Sensitive Attributes

These are the attributes that individuals do not want to reveal about themselves. Examples can be salary, relationship statuses and diseases.

2.1.4 Non-Sensitive Attributes

These are the attributes other than the above mentioned 3 types. They may not have a direct or indirect relationship to identify individuals.

Any PPDP process should include a mechanism to identify these attributes related to personal data before applying any sanitization technique. Based on the nature of the attribute, different sanitization techniques must be applied.

2.2 Existing Data Sanitization Techniques

Many research works have been carried out to come up with various sanitization techniques to protect personal data (Mehta and Rao, 2015; Fung et al., 2010)

2.2.1 Suppression

This mechanism replaces some attribute values by a symbol like '*' to indicate those attributes are repressed. For instance, a credit card number can be suppressed as 34** **** ****.

2.2.2 Generalization

This implies replacing an attribute with a generalized value of its class, for instance male and female values of the gender attribute or a nationality attribute can be replaced with 'Any' which is a more general value. Generalization makes sure that a combined set of quasi identifiers cannot be used to uniquely identify a person after generalizing.

2.2.3 Swapping

As the name implies this includes swapping some attribute values. For example, swapping the gender values of two records.

2.2.4 Anatomization

This involves separating quasi identifiers and sensitive attributes into different tables so that the relationship among them will be broken.

2.2.5 Permutation

This is about creating groups or buckets based on quasi identifiers and then shuffle the values of their respective sensitive attributes in each group to break the relationship between quasi identifier and the sensitive attributes.

2.2.6 Perturbation

This is about replacing the original values of some sensitive attributes using some fake values.

Table 1 shows some health records which contain different types of attributes mentioned above. Name can be considered as a direct identifier where age, gender, zip code and nationality can be considered as quasi identifiers. These direct identifiers and quasi identifiers can be used to recognize diseases different individuals have without their consent and diseases can be something these individuals don't want to reveal.

	Age	Gender	Zip Code	Nationality	Disease
John	28	M	13053	Russian	Heart Disease
Jack	29	M	13055	Chinese	Heart Disease
Bruce	22	M	13061	Japanese	Heart Disease
Ann	24	F	14332	Russian	Heart Disease
Lewis	41	M	14556	American	Cancer
Richard	45	M	13227	American	Cancer
Anders	50	M	13226	American	Cancer
Paul	37	M	13221	American	Flu
Janet	34	F	13229	American	Flu
Cary	56	M	13225	American	Flu

Table 1: Health records

Table 2 shows the application of different sanitization techniques to identifiers so that it is difficult to distinguish individuals from each other. For age, gender and nationality columns, generalization is applied whereas for the zip code column, suppression is applied.

	Age	Gender	Zip Code	Nationality	Disease
******	20-29	Any	130**	Any	Heart Disease
******	20-29	Any	130**	Any	Heart Disease
******	20-29	Any	130**	Any	Heart Disease
******	20-29	Any	14***	Any	Heart Disease
******	40-59	Any	14***	American	Cancer
******	40-59	Any	1322*	American	Cancer
******	40-59	Any	1322*	American	Cancer
******	30-39	Any	1322*	American	Flu
******	30-39	Any	1322*	American	Flu
******	40-59	Any	1322*	American	Flu

Table 2: Sanitized health records

2.3 Existing Privacy Models

As privacy is a very subjective concept there should be some baseline models to measure it against. Research community has come up with such benchmarks over time.

2.3.1 K-anonymity

A set of data is said to have k-anonymity property if the information for each individual cannot be eminently differentiated from at least k - 1 other individuals who are in the same dataset (Samarati and Sweeny, 1998).

2.3.2 L-diversity

This is an extension to the k-anonymity model, which diminishes the granularity of data using mechanisms including generalization and suppression. This tries to overcome a couple of weak points of the k-anonymity model (Machanavajjhala et al., 2006). If the variability of sensitive attributes is little, then it is possible to recognize individuals with some background knowledge, even though the data is k anonymized. L-diversity tries to solve this by setting a rule on distinct number of sensitive values an equivalence class (the set of records with similar quasi identifier values after anonymizing) can have.

2.3.3 T-closeness

This is an enhancement to l-diversity model to overcome its flows. Further reduction using this causes some loss of usefulness of the data as it tries to distort data (Li et al., 2007). This tries to find solutions for the problems of semantic closeness and skewness of data, that are not addressed by l-diversity model.

Any system which is intended to adopt a privacy preserving process should adhere to a couple of steps.

- Extract personal privacy related attributes from the data
- Sanitize those extracted attributes using a sanitization mechanism that suits the nature of the attribute
- Evaluate the level of privacy using privacy measures
- Evaluate the level of utility or usefulness using utility measures

But this process becomes very challenging if the data is unstructured, due to a couple of reasons.

2.4 Challenges with Textual, Unstructured Social Media Data

Social media has become an essential part of people's life. There are many prevailing social media platforms that tend to connect individuals forming complex networks. And the number of users who actively participate in these platforms are drastically increasing over time pumping a huge amount of data in a high velocity. This obviously creates challenges for data scientists.

People are not reluctant anymore to share their personal information on the world wide web. Even though they don't consider the privacy aspects a lot at the point of sharing, no one will prefer any sensitive information about their privacy being compromised.

There is various analysis that can be done on top of social media data to derive many interesting patterns. Facebook status analysis and Twitter's tweet analysis are two such analysis that involve unstructured data. Obviously, these data involve so many sensitive facts about individuals. Unstructured nature of these data makes the privacy preservation more difficult. For example, think about the following sentence.

"My teacher who lived in Corktown died of cancer yesterday at age 65"

Even though this sentence does not contain any names or direct identifiers of an individual, the details provided there such as occupation, city and age can be used to disclose the individual. So, the things shared on social media can reveal many personal information indirectly. Ensuring this kind of data does not reveal any personal information has some inherent challenges.

- Extracting personal information related attributes from unstructured data is not straight forward
- Sanitization techniques cannot be directly applied on unstructured data
- As social media is a huge platform of information for analysis, any privacy preservation technique should not corrupt its original value, so that data will be useless
- As social media falls into big data category, any PPDP framework should cater to the challenges like variety, volume and velocity

3. Related Work

Privacy preserving data publishing is being a topic of interest in the research community for a long time now. But the advancements in digitization and computing introduces new challenges in the area of privacy preserving data publishing too. This section describes a couple of related work in the context of PPDP and unstructured data.

Fung et al. have done a comprehensive survey on the topical developments of privacy preserving data publishing techniques. They have discussed about the current status of privacy preservation and highlighted the fact that it's getting more and more attention over time. They have thoroughly discussed about anonymization techniques such as generalization and suppression, anatomization and permutation, and perturbation etc. Additionally, they have highlighted mechanisms to preserve privacy in a way that the data will remain practically useful. They talk about various information metrics that can be used to measure data usefulness such as special purpose metrics, general purpose metrics and trade-off metrics. A couple of existing anonymization algorithms are brought forward in this research, and they are classified into a set of subsets, based on the underlying methodology – whether it is based on record linkage, table linkage or attribute linkage (Fung et al., 2010).

Ramya et al. present an attempt to do privacy preserving data publishing on unstructured data with a somewhat different approach. They too have understood the fact that it is challenging to apply traditional PPDP techniques when the dataset it semi/unstructured. They have followed a document classification approach to categorize documents to indicate whether a document contains sensitive information or not. Before doing the actual classification, documents are preprocessed to remove any stop words and do the stemming. They have used a boolean label called Sensitivity Disclosure Label (SDL) to indicate a document contains sensitive information or not. Two different classifiers are employed to do the document classification. They are Multinomial Naive Bayes and K-Nearest Neighbor classifiers. As the dataset for model building and verification, they have used i2b2 (Informatics for Integrating Biology & the Bedside) medical dataset. In this approach they are only concerned about the domain level document classification, but not about a detailed tagging where the content inside the documents can be sanitized (Ramya et al., 2019).

Gardner et al. have described in their paper, an approach to de-identify unstructured medical data. They try to fill in some gaps in the privacy preservation techniques of current medical data domain. The scholars argue that current methodologies mainly consider simple anonymization techniques without taking the full advantage of the already done research work. So, they come up with an integrated framework, which embeds many powerful privacy preservation mechanisms. They employ a Bayesian classifier with a sampling-based technique and a conditional random field-based classifier to extract sensitive information from medical data. And, a k-anonymity based model is used for de-identifying information at the same time maintaining maximum data usefulness. As further work, they mention that we can explore into a mechanism where we can prioritize attributes based on their relatedness to the privacy. And extracting indirect identifiers like quasi identifiers are not focused under this research (Gardner and Xiong, 2009).

Thavavel et al. come up with another framework which talks about privacy preservation in a distributed environment with unstructured data. The proposed approach is about converting unstructured data to structured data before applying any privacy preservation mechanisms. They have converted the unstructured data to XML and then mapped that XML to node representation and the outcome is structured data. A distributed mechanism which vertically partitions the heterogeneous data are proposed under this mechanism. Data volume becomes a constraint here again, as it's not practical to convert a large amount of unstructured data to structured data (Thavavel and Sivakumar, 2012).

Liu et al. propose a privacy preserving middleware called LinkMirage which controls privacy preservation of social relationships. They claim that their novel algorithm de-identify the social relationship graph and at the same time it does not distort graph utility or usefulness. They have done an analysis using a huge real-world Google+ dataset which contained 940 million links. And they claim that the proposed algorithm guarantee 10x privacy preservation compared to the existing research work. This algorithm mainly depends on perturbation mechanisms (Liu and Mittal, 2016).

4. Methodology

Figure 1 summarizes the overall process adopted in the proposed methodology. The suggested approach mainly consists of a Twitter data publisher, a privacy preserving middleware and privacy and utility evaluator. The purpose of the implementation was to come up with an end to end system which can realize the concept of privacy preserving data publishing for unstructured and textual social media data. Each of these modules will be discussed in this section.

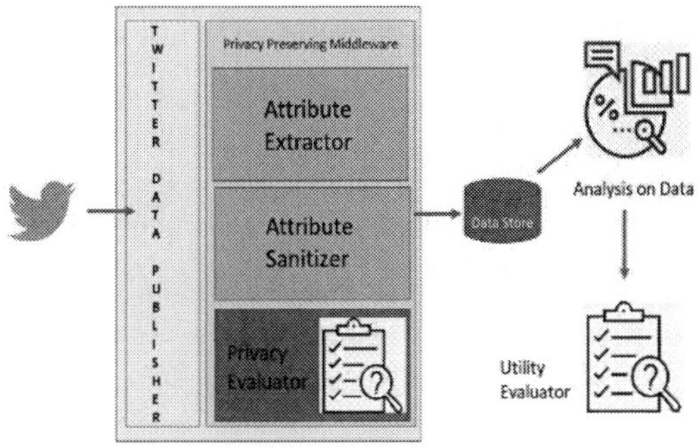

Figure 1: Overall system architecture.

4.1 Twitter Data Publisher

A data publisher was implemented as the main source of test data generating for the solution. This is a Python program which can perform a keyword search via the Twitter API to extract some tweets, or through which the users can push a precompiled set of tweets into the system. This will be the entry point in the developed prototype.

4.2 Privacy Attribute Extractor

This is the most critical module in the prototype. A decision tree-based tagging model was developed to tag tweets with attributes related to personal information. Figure 2 shows the methodology adopted in training the tagger. The manually tagged corpus was transformed before it was fed to the decision tree classifier.

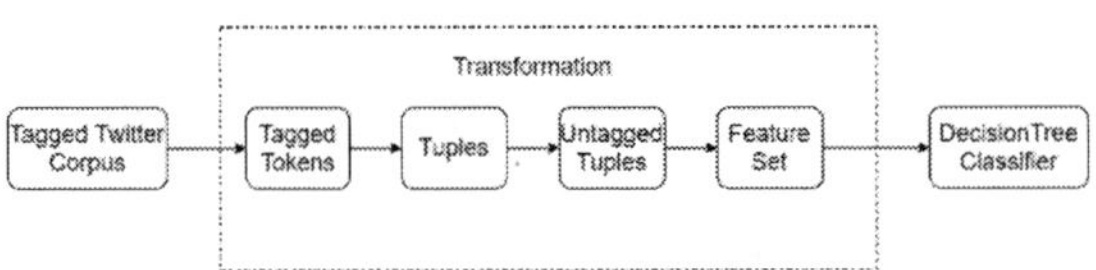

Figure 2: Data transformation.

A data set of 3000 tweets were manually annotated by 3 annotators for different identifiers related to privacy to build a corpus. The annotation scheme is described in table 3.

Attribute Type	Tag	Attribute
Direct Identifiers	DI	Name, TwitterId
Quasi Identifiers	QIAGE	Age
Quasi Identifiers	QIRACE	Race
Quasi Identifiers	QIREGION	Region
Quasi Identifiers	QIGENDER	Gender
Quasi Identifiers	QILANG	Language
Quasi Identifiers	QIJOB	Occupation
Sensitive Attribute	SA	Health Conditions, Relationship Status, Salary, Political Preferences
Non-Sensitive Attribute	NONE	Anything that does not belong to above

Table 3: Annotation scheme

This corpus was preprocessed and transformed before being fed into the decision tree classifier for training. The transformation utilities contained methods for tokenizing, untagging and extracting features from the words.

A set of syntactic, orthographic, gazetteer and affix features were used in the transformation process. Table 4 shows all the features extracted in the process.

Feature	Feature Type
is_first	Orthographic
is_last	Orthographic
is_capitalized	Orthographic
is_all_caps	Orthographic
is_all_lower	Orthographic
prefix-1	Affix
prefix-2	Affix
prefix-3	Affix
suffix-1	Affix
suffix-2	Affix
suffix-3	Affix
prev_word	Orthographic
next_word	Orthographic
has_hyphen	Orthographic
is_numeric	Orthographic
pos_tag	Syntactic
named_entity	Gazetteer

Table 4: Features selected

Insights for features were obtained by a named entity extractor that was built using AdaBoost (Carreras and Marques, 2003). As gazetteer features, values suggested by spaCy's named entity recognition are used (spaCy.io, 2016).

Then this transformed dataset was input into the classifier and trained. Train and test data were split based on the 70:30 rule and the confusion matrix was computed to score the model. This brings a macro average of 0.74 for the F1 score. Accuracy stays at 0.92 as the result is highly impacted by the 'none' label proportion.

	Precision	Recall	F1-Score
DI	0.83	0.7	0.76
QIAGE	0.69	0.77	0.73
QIGENDER	0.57	0.65	0.61
QIRACE	0.74	0.49	0.6
QIREGION	0.78	0.82	0.8
QIJOB	0.59	0.7	0.64
SA	0.73	0.81	0.77
NONE	0.98	0.98	0.98

Table 5: Classifier confusion metrics

Following is a sample tweet automatically tagged through the tagging model.

('My', 'None')('teacher', 'QIJOB')('who', 'None')('lived', 'None')('in', 'None')('USA', 'QIREGION')('died', 'None')('of', 'None')('cancer', 'SA')('at', 'None')('age', 'None')('65', 'QIAGE')

All the new tweets published through the data publisher will go through this module and get automatically tagged with appropriate tags.

4.3 Privacy Attribute Sanitizer

The next module in the privacy preserving pipeline is attribute sanitizer. This incorporates some sanitization techniques from the literature that suits the nature of each identifier. Sanitization Techniques applied to each attribute is presented in table 6.

Attribute	Sanitization Technique	Origina l Value	Sanitized Value
Name, TwitterId	Complete Anonymization	John	******
Age	Generalization (to a number range)	65	60-70
Race	Union	Indian	American, Indian, African
Region	Union	Sri Lanka	India, Sri Lanka, America, Germany, Canada
Gender	Generalization	Female	Any
Language	Generalization	English	Any
Occupation	Swapping	Teacher	Doctor

Table 6: Sanitization scheme

After applying the sanitization techniques on the tagged sentence, the original tweet is rebuilt with the anonymized values. Following shows how the above tagged tweet looks after applying anonymization techniques.

"My doctor who lived in India, Sri Lanka, USA, Canada died of Cancer at the age of 60-70."

Name	Age	Gender	Zip Code	Nationality	Disease
Ann	20-29	Any	130**	Any	Heart Disease
Bruce	20-29	Any	130**	Any	Heart Disease
James	20-29	Any	130**	Any	Viral Infection
Janet	20-29	Any	130**	Any	Viral Infection
Fox	40-59	Any	14***	Asian	Cancer
Richard	40-59	Any	14***	Asian	Flu
Anders	40-59	Any	14***	Asian	Cancer
Paul	40-59	Any	14***	Asian	Flu
Helen	30-39	Any	1322*	American	Cancer
Cary	30-39	Any	1322*	American	Cancer
John	30-39	Any	1322*	American	Cancer
Jack	30-39	Any	1322*	American	Cancer

Equivalence Class

4-Anonymous Data Set

Figure 3: A 4-anonymized data set.

The developed prototype provides the ability to do the anonymization in two ways.

1. Simple anonymizing: Under this category all the quasi identifiers and direct identifiers will be anonymized without considering the fact to which extent they contribute to revealing the privacy.
2. K-anonymizing: Under this category, anonymization will be performed according to the k-anonymity model where the user can specify the k value. According to k-anonymity model, dataset is divided into equivalence classes based on similar quasi identifiers and the objective is to anonymize data in a way, a record can't be distinguished from other records in its equivalence class. Figure 3 shows an example of a 4-anonymized data set where each record is not distinguishable from 4-1 other records. Increasing the value of k strengthens the privacy. But it can be challenging to find the correct k value which can preserve the privacy at the same time protects the utility.

The above anonymization mechanisms can be applied on either a single tweet or a set of tweets. If it is a single tweet, simple anonymization will be applied and if it is a set of tweets, user can select between simple anonymization and k-anonymization.

Textual dataset is converted into the form of structured data to perform k-anonymization and after doing the anonymization, the textual dataset is rebuilt using the structured dataset. Figure 4 shows how tweets look when they are converted to the structured format.

AgeGender	Job	Region	SA	CountRows	
she,25M		,East		4	1,2,3,4
she,25M		,East	Cancer	1	5
she,25M		,East	cancer	3	6,7,8
He,Aunt		Bhilwara...,@BoSnerdleycameos		2	25,26
He,Aunt		Bhilwara...,@BoSnerdleycancer		4	23,45,47,48
He,Aunt		Bhilwara...,@BoSnerdleycauses		1	24
He,man		Omaha..	Cancer	4	34,35,36,37

Figure 4: Textual data that are converted to structured format and k-anonymized

4.4 Utility Evaluator

A couple of metrics are provided to evaluate the quality or the utility of the privacy preserved dataset. These measures specifically target the quality of the quasi identifier groups.

4.4.1 Discernibility Metric (DM)

This assigns a penalty to each tuple based on how many other tuples in the database are indistinguishable from it (Fung et al, 2010). If a record belongs to qid group of size n, then the penalty for the record will be n and the penalty for the group will be n^2. Whenever an anonymization task is performed, user is given the ability to calculate the discernibility metrics for each quasi identifier. The specialty with discernibility metric is it can compare the cost of generalizing for each qid value. Higher the discernibility value, higher the cost of generalization is.

4.4.2 Loss Metric (LM)

This calculates the normalized loss of each attribute of every tuple. This, in particular targets the information loss caused by the generalization. LM is defined as the number of nodes a record's value has been made indistinguishable from (via generalization) compared to the total number of original leaf nodes in the taxonomy tree (Fung et al, 2010). Loss metric is created as n-1/m where n is the number of descendants of a parent value in a generalization tree and m is the total number of domain values of an attribute.

4.4.3 Generalization Counting

This counts how many generalization/suppression operations were performed.

5. Dataset

The dataset developed for tagging the tweets is one of the biggest achievements of this research. The research community was lacking a dataset which has annotated textual data for privacy related attributes. One of the greatest intentions of this research was to come up with an annotated corpus including tweets, which can be used for future privacy preserving tasks and that goal was successfully achieved.

Tweets to build the corpus was selectively picked from a public Kaggle dataset based on a keyword search (Kaggle, 2018). This dataset contains 3000 tweets which are annotated adhering to the scheme shown in Table 3 using 3 annotators. These attributes are subjective; therefore, the tweets were cross annotated by each annotator and an agreement study was performed. The average kappa values lie between 0.6-0.7 proving our dataset is reliable.

6. Experimental Results

A keyword search was performed on Twitter using Twitter's public API to create an experimental data set. A couple of sensitive attribute values like 'cancer', 'lesbian' and 'gay' were used as keywords and a dataset of 1000 tweets were created. Then both simple anonymization and k-anonymization were performed on this tweet set and utility metrics were computed. The objective of this experiment was to simulate a real-life data anonymization operation. K value used was 4.

First the no. of sanitizations was counted, and a percentage of sanitized terms were measured.

Total number of terms sanitized: 334 (simple anonymization)
Percentage of terms sanitized: 7.7% (simple anonymization)
Total number of terms sanitized: 303 (k-anonymization)
Percentage of terms sanitized: 7.1% (k-anonymization)

Table 7: Sanitization counts

Table 8 summarizes the discernibility metric values for each quasi identifier type.

Quasi Identifier Group	Anonymized Value	DM	Privacy Type
QIGENDER	Any	9025	Simple Anonymization
QIREGION	Any	6084	Simple Anonymization
QIGENDER	She, Men, Women	4900	k-Anonymization
	Girl, Woman	64	
	Girlgriend, Girl	49	
	Girl	64	
QIREGION	Hollywood	9	k-Anonymization

Table 8: DM values for different attributes

First two records of table 8 show the DM values for gender and region under simple anonymization. An interpretation for those two results will be the cost of generalization of gender is higher than cost of generalization of region. At the same time, we can say that more originally distinguishable values have become indistinguishable under region generalization, but at a lesser cost.

Figure 5 shows the DM variation within a quasi-identifier and how each generalization has costed. Through that we can get an idea about what are the costliest generalizations.

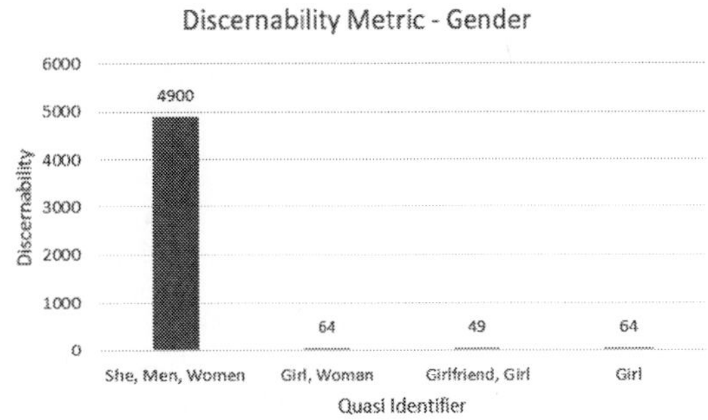

Figure 5: Discernibility metrics – gender.

And also, if we closely look at the values of the qid groups, we can understand the fact that the tagger is performing very well with extracting attributes as all the attributes depicted in the graphs/tables are meaningful in their category.

Table 9 summarizes the loss metric values for each qid attribute. For the sample validation dataset used loss metric seems to be close to 0.8 for both the privacy types. Sanitization count and DM values seem slightly lower for k-anonymization than simple anonymization, but LM values are almost equal for both privacy types.

Quasi Identifier Group	LM	QID values	Privacy Type
QIGENDER	0.83	She, he, girls, men, girlfriends, shemales	Simple Anonymization
QIREGION	0.75	Odisha, China, Narsipatnam, Africa	Simple Anonymization
QIGENDER	0.86	Girl, women, girlfriend, woman, girls, men, she	k-Anonymization
QIREGION	0.8	Hollywood, Carmel, Delhi, Sindh, China	k-Anonymization

Table 9: LM values for different qids

The prototype enables the user to perform the anonymization operation and calculate these metrics through the framework itself to get a better idea.

7. Discussion and Future Work

This research has focused on building a privacy preserving data publishing middleware for textual, unstructured social media data and has successfully achieved that objective. As an additional contribution to the research community, this research has developed a reliable dataset with annotated tweets for privacy related attributes. In order to measure the usability of the newly generated data, utility metric calculation is embedded as a part of the framework. And specifically, this framework supports simple anonymization and k-anonymization which are very popular in the research community to preserve privacy of structured data. Therefore, this research can be considered as an integration of traditional privacy preserving approaches to textual and unstructured data in a novel way.

As future work, the framework can be enhanced by introducing some innovative features.

- As the tagger built in this research relies on a decision tree-based approach, some different approaches can be tried out using sequence tagging mechanisms to improve the accuracy.
- The dataset can be enhanced with introducing tweets with other different quasi identifiers than the ones used in this research
- User can be given the ability to define the attributes that are important to them, forming the foundation to personalized privacy

8. Conclusion

The core objective of this research was to come up with a novel framework, that can preserve the privacy of unstructured, textual social media data before publishing to any analytical platform. In order to achieve this task, a dataset was created and tagged with privacy related attribute tags. This dataset can be utilized by the research community to perform privacy preserving tasks on unstructured data in the future as well. This research comes up with an end to end framework for privacy preserving data publishing of unstructured data, including steps like attribute extraction, attribute sanitization and utility evaluation. The main attribute extraction module comes up with a F1 score of 0.7 for most of the quasi identifiers. Additionally, some points for improvement and promising future work too are discussed in this paper.

9. Ethics Statement

The dataset created in the research was built selectively based on a publicly available Kaggle dataset and it is not targeting any specific individual. Intermediate results containing personal data of any anonymization job will not be persisted for future use. The concept and research work are fully independent and impartial.

10. Bibliographical References

Alaphilippe A., Gizikis A., Hanot C., Automated tackling of disinformation, 2019.

Bu Y., Fu A.W.C., Wong R.C.W., Chen L., Li J., Preserving serial data publishing by role composition, in Proc. Very Large Database Endowment, 2008, pp. 845–856.

Carreras X., Marquez L., Padro L., A Simple Named Entity Extractor using AdaBoost, in Proc. Conference on Computational Natural Language Learning, 2003.

Chen B.C., Kifer D., LeFevre K., Machanavajjhala A. Privacy-preserving data publishing, in Proc. Foundations and Trends in Databases Conference, 2009, pp. 1 – 167.

Duan Y., Wang J., Kam M., and Canny J. Privacy preserving link analysis on dynamic weighted graph in Computational & Mathematical Organization Theory, 2005, pp.141–159

Fan L., Jin H., A Practical Framework for Privacy Preserving Data Analytics, in Proc. 24th International Conference on World Wide Web, 2015.

Fung B.C.M., Wang K., Philip S.Y., Introduction to Privacy-preserving Data Publishing: Concepts and Techniques. Boca Raton: CRC Press, 2010.

Fung B.C.M., Wang K., Chen R., and Yu P. S., Privacy preserving data publishing: A survey on recent developments, in ACM Computing Surveys, 2010, pp. 14:1 – 14:53

Gardner J. and Xiong L., An integrated framework for deidentifying heterogeneous data, in Proc. Data and Knowledge Engineering, 2009, pp. 1441-1451.

General Data Protection Regulation [Online]. Available: https://en.wikipedia.org/wiki/General_Data_Protection_Regulation

Industrial-Strength Natural Language Processing [Online]. Available: https://spacy.io/

Li N., Li T., Venkatasubramanian S., t-Closeness: Beyond k-Anonymity and l-Diversity, in IEEE 23rd International Conference on Data Engineering, 2007.

Liu C., Mittal P. Linkmirage: Enabling privacy preserving analytics on social relationships, in NDSS, 2016, pp. 21-24.

Liu K., Das K., Grandison T., and Kargupta H. preserving data analysis on graphs and social networks, In H. Kargupta, J. Han, P. Yu, R. Motwani, and V. Kumar, editors, Next Generation Data Mining. CRC Press, 2008.

Machanavajjhala A., Gehrke J., Kifer D., Venkitasubramaniam M., l-diversity: Privacy beyond kanonymity, in Proc. 22nd International Conference on Data Engineering (ICDE). IEEE Computer Society, 2006.

Mehta B., Rao U., Privacy preserving unstructured big data analytics – issues and challenges, in Proc. International Conference on Security and Privacy, Nagpur, India, 2015, pp. 120-124.

Mendes R., Vilela J.P, Privacy-preserving data mining: Methods, metrics, and applications, in IEEE Access, 2017, pp. 10562–10582.

Number of social media users worldwide from 2010 to 2021 (in billions) [Online]. Available: https://www.statista.com/statistics/278414/number-ofworldwide-social-network-users/

Samarati P., Sweeney L., Protecting privacy when disclosing information: k-anonymity and its enforcement through generalization and cell suppression, Technical report, SRI International, 1998.

Thavavel V., Sivakumar S., A generalized Framework of Privacy Preservation in Distributed Data mining for Unstructured Data Environment, in International Journal of Computer Science Issues, 2012, pp. 434-441.

The "localization" of Russian citizens' personal data [Online]. Available:https://home.kpmg/be/en/home/insights/2018/09/the-localisation-of-russian-citizens-personal-data.html

11. Language Resource References

Twitter Sentiment Analysis [Online]. Available: https://www.kaggle.com/paoloripamonti/twitter-sentiment-analysis

Proceedings of the Workshop on Social Threats in Online Conversations: Understanding and Management (STOC-2020), pages 29–34
Language Resources and Evaluation Conference (LREC 2020), Marseille, 11–16 May 2020

Information Space Dashboard

Theresa Krumbiegel, Albert Pritzkau, Hans-Christian Schmitz
Fraunhofer Institute for Communication, Information Processing and Ergonomics FKIE
Fraunhofer Str. 20, 53343 Wachtberg, Germany
{theresa.krumbiegel, albert.pritzkau, hans-christian.schmitz}@fkie.fraunhofer.de

Abstract

The information space, where information is generated, stored, exchanged and discussed, is not idyllic but a space where campaigns of disinformation and destabilization are conducted. Such campaigns are subsumed under the terms "hybrid warfare" and "information warfare" (Woolley and Howard, 2017). In order to enable awareness of them, we propose an information space dashboard comprising various components/apps for data collection, analysis and visualization. The aim of the dashboard is to support an analyst in generating a common operational picture of the information space, link it with an operational picture of the physical space and, thus, contribute to overarching situational awareness. The dashboard is work in progress. However, a first prototype with components for exploiting elementary language statistics, keyword and metadata analysis, text classification and network analysis has been implemented. Further components, in particular, for event extraction and sentiment analysis are under development. As a demonstration case, we briefly discuss the analysis of historical data regarding violent anti-migrant protests and respective counter-protests that took place in Chemnitz in 2018.
Keywords: Information Space, Hybrid Warfare, Machine Learning

1. Introduction

In civilian emergency response and disaster management as well as in military operations, situation awareness is based on observation and orientation, and it is a necessary precondition for decision and action (Boyd, 1975). In order to reach situational awareness, information has to be collected and fed into a common operational picture. The picture comprises a representation of the actual situation as well as planned or predicted future events. Based on the operational picture, the situation can be accessed, the possibilities of own actions can be estimated, respective plans can be developed and decisions can be taken. Last but not least, own activities can be monitored and controlled.

With the advent of the once-so-called "new" media, in particular social media, the information space has become an additional domain, in which situational awareness must be reached. The information space is linked to the physical world, as it contributes to the creation of (the common picture of) reality: negotiations take place on which information counts as factual and which doesn't, which events are considered to be "real" and how they are to be assessed, which prognoses shall be believed and which not, whom one can trust and whom one cannot. Moreover, planning and preparation of events in the physical world take place: individuals and groups are mobilized for actions, which can be as diverse as demonstrations, riots or spontaneous help in emergency situations.

It is therefore not surprising, that the information space has become a theatre of operations in its own right: on the one hand, actors can try to destabilize a society and mobilize the population for their own purposes by means of propaganda and disinformation campaigns. For such aggressive activities, the term "hybrid warfare" has been coined. On the other hand, activities within the information space can be necessary to approach a population, inform it on the situation and the measures to be taken and, thus, stabilize a society. Such activities come under the umbrella of an "integrated approach" as it is followed by the European Union, among others (Schmitz et al., 2019).

The concepts of situational awareness and a common operational picture are not as elaborated and clear for the information space as they are for the physical domain. Our aim is to contribute to the sharpening of the concepts. We do so with a bottom-up approach, namely by developing means for creating various views on aspects of the information space and thus providing elements of an operational picture. To this end, we propose an information space dashboard as an analyst's working environment, which comes with a toolbox for information analysis. An operational picture of the information space will be different from one of the physical space. Therefore, systems for supporting situational awareness will substantially differ: an information space dashboard cannot just be an adapted command and control information system (C2IS) with a map-view as its core element.

Within this paper, we will firstly refer to related work, then outline a prototype of an information space dashboard and its components, describe a demonstration case, and, finally, conclude by summing up the results, name open issues and discuss obvious ethical questions.

2. Related Work

Bergh (2019) discusses the need of the detection of influence operations on social media: "over the past few years national defence organisations have received a wakeup call with regard to social media and their use to attempt to manipulate opinion, whether in hybrid conflicts [...] or in low-level societal manipulation". This had already been emphasized by Franke (2011) who pointed out that Social Media campaigns do not derive from one specific source, but can be conducted by a number of various actors, including foreign and domestic governments as well as activist groups. The targets can be as diverse and are not limited to one specific group or individual. Examples that bear witness to this fact are cases of computational propaganda during the 2016 US Presidential Election, the influence political bots had on the 2016 Brexit referendum and bot networks as well as computational propaganda that played a role in the 2014

presidential election, the constitutional crisis and impeachment process in Brazil (Woolley and Howard, 2017).
Bergh (2019) poses requirements and challenges regarding the development of a software solution to support the detection of influence operations. Requirements are in particular flexibility, interoperability for information sharing between different operators and the ability to respond rapidly to changing situations. Challenges are the organisational and technical patchwork, limitations of resources like computing power and storage, heterogeneity of data and (entitled) privacy concerns. These are to be considered in the process of developing an information space dashboard.
Beside this, the analysis of social media data has become a constant field of research. An important topic, among others, is the detection of threats and hate speech in online conversations with the help of machine learning algorithms. Colbaugh and Glass (2012) and Lerman and Hogg (2012) are to be named as examples for works in this domain.
To capture the information space, Information Extraction (IE) from vast amounts of unstructured data needs to be implemented. Li et al. (2019) developed a system for multilingual knowledge extraction that is able to perform entity discovery and linking, time expression extraction and normalization, relation extraction, event extraction and event coreference. Such a tool is invaluable in the context of comprehending the information space and should be considered during the development of the dashboard. We further refer to this in chapter 5. Liu et al. (2019) introduce a technique to mange data accumulations by means of synthesis. Even though the described approach focuses on the processing of Chinese text data, methods such as the finding of subtopics and the synthesis of news articles could be transferred to data written in other languages, for example German.
Another aim of the information space dashboard is the identification of disinformation (campaigns). As can be seen in subchapter 5.2., we already conducted research in the field of fake news detection. However, we can not disregard insights from other researches. Nadeem et al. (2019), for example, present an automatic end-to-end fact checking system (FAKTA). FAKTA incorporates document retrieval, stance detection, evidence extraction and linguistic analysis in order to predict the factuality of claims.

3. Information Space

In the general understanding, the information space includes all technology-enhanced communication, coordination, and collaboration services that facilitate the creation, sharing, and exchange of information and ideas within communities of interest. The creation of such communities is a fundamental characteristic of social media, they form quickly and enable effective communication. Though these communities are only virtual, they are usually no less robust than the physical communities in which we live. In many ways they are even more robust as spatial and temporal boundaries are removed. Social media services, in particular, promote the exchange of information between members of a community in a way that encourages contributions of content improving collaboration, knowledge-sharing and engagement. The information space is increasingly being used as an information source, including information related to national and global security.
Exploitation of the information space generally has three fundamental objectives: information discovery, situational awareness enhancement and predictive analysis. Capabilities in addressing these objectives provide essential estimates of potential risks faced by communities, economies and the environment. When exploiting media sources, analysis is commonly limited to two aspects: users as basic units of the network and content as basic elements of communication (Kwak et al., 2010). These two aspects themselves are already invaluable sources of information. However, social networks additionally offer the context of communication and interaction represented by the network itself, namely, the network topology in the form of entities and relations. In addition to content, a given network structure promotes the derivation of activity and process patterns which can significantly improve situational awareness (Helbing et al., 2014).

4. Social Sensing Capabilities

In social networks, humans are central in the sensing process. Social media services, in particular, provide a rich and flexible platform for performing mining processes with different kinds of data such as text documents, images, audio and video files. In the context of this paper, we consider online sites and applications which consist of users, social links, and interactive communications as data sources. These social media services can be seen as a subset of social media that includes a social network of some kind. Social networks are transforming into inherently multi-modal data sources. In recent years, sensor data collection techniques and services have been integrated into many kinds of social networks and have increased the richness of the data collection process in the context of the network structure. Furthermore, it renewed interest in the study of collective dynamics, and in particular the study of individual mobility patterns in addition to social relations. We envision that the whole phenomenon of social networks will continue to evolve quickly as digital technology increasingly penetrates the realm of the physical world, providing new research challenges for information systems, and especially for our dashboard approach. Since most current social network services usually implement only simple models of a social network, it should be noted that these models cannot mirror the richness of real world complexity. But even abstract representations of social dynamics have proved to be useful in acquiring knowledge for decision making and in supporting pro-active intervention before critical events occur.

5. Analysis & Visualization

Analysis involves reviewing and assessing large collections of information by means of complex processes of analytical reasoning, hypothesis formulation, and decision making. The analysis process itself is inherently iterative, involving alternating narrowing and broadening of focus, and is often performed as an exploratory search for relevant information. With the dashboard approach, we attempt to analyze the information space by emphasizing different data representations. Diverse representations of data support the

exploratory search beyond predictable fact retrieval by enabling various levels of abstraction that can be applied to different problems, questions, tasks or stages of the analysis.
Both content and interactions, as introduced in chapter 3., are considered for the purpose of discovering actionable patterns and understanding human behaviour. To understand some characteristics of typical accounts, or of the overall network and its potential reach, the most basic metrics – e.g. the number of followers and following and patterns of tweeting – serve as a starting point. These metrics, as the result of elementary language statistics, already provide appropriate controls for specifying the data and views of interest. Controls enable analysts to selectively represent the data, to filter out unrelated information, and to sort information to expose patterns. Quantitative information derived from the input data such as normalized values, statistical summaries, and aggregates, serve as additional descriptive features to support the analysis.
Traditional information discovery methods are based on content: documents, terms, and the relationships between them (Leskovec and Lang, 2008). Emergent social network services, however, allow for a range of extended features for aggregating content, attributes, and social graphs and take advantage of this newly formed environment of user-generated content. Complex relationships between content and people represented in social applications must be leveraged in order to recognize activities, events, groups and trends. Indeed, it has been observed that the use of a combination of social structure and different kinds of data can be a very powerful tool for mining purposes (Qi et al., 2012).
Beyond quantitative features we can rely on a number of methods for IE which take natural language texts as input and produce structured information specified by certain criteria. Various sub-tasks of IE such as Named Entity Recognition, Coreference Resolution, Named Entity Linking, Relation Extraction and Knowledge Base reasoning form the building blocks of a complex language understanding task. Many of these methods such as text categorization referred to in 5.2. or sentiment prediction referred to in 5.5. usually reframe this complex language understanding task as a simpler sequence or token classification problem.
The analysis process is usually based on various preprocessing steps preceding the presentation in the dashboard.

5.1. Elementary Language Statistics

Quantitative analysis of texts can serve the exploratory investigation of online media as they can reveal trends and topics under discussion. To these statistical means belong frequency distributions of content words plotted in various ways, extraction of key words and key phrases, and analysis of metadata, including hash tags, among others, as "the hashtags used by 'ordinary' Twitter members construct their position as commentators on cultural events produced by others" (Page, 2012).

5.2. Text Clustering and Classification

Text can be clustered and/or classified according to stylistic surface phenomena which are significantly correlated with semantic or pragmatic properties of interest. Text clustering can give rise to the topics under discussion.
We successfully conducted experiments with a so-called "fake news" filter. This filter is actually a classifier that exploits specific syntactic constructions, word choices and elements of hate speech which have been proven significant by an exploratory investigation into disinformation campaigns. These features can be used to recognize potential (!) fake news articles (Schade et al., 2018; Pritzkau, 2019). The methodology does not come without questions, however, as the extraction of language-related features can establish a bias against specific types of authors. If the features are, e.g., significant for usage of the German language by native Russian speakers – cf. (Böttger, 2008; Gladrow, 1998) – the system will automatically assign a higher "fake news" probability to articles written by Russians.

5.3. Network Analysis

To identify the communicative and interactive behavior of a user in a social network, and to detect which behaviors are unusual and might therefore hint at a bot-like behavior, it is worthwhile to analyze associated metadata. A bot becomes noticeable by the controlled character of its activity in the information space. Through metadata, it is possible to represent structures at the micro and macro level that reveal such controlled activities.
The micro level is concerned with the identification of nodes and their connection in the network. Nodes represent individual Twitter accounts whose interaction with each other can be shown by edges connecting them. Patterns that emerge in the micro structure of a social network give insights into its prevailing macro structure.

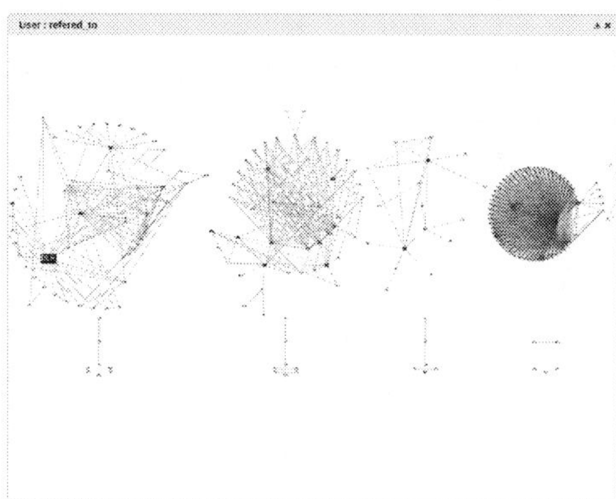

Figure 1: Reference Behavior in a Social Network

Figure 1 shows an example of referencing behavior in a social network. We see the user accounts as nodes and references (@-mention) between them as edges. The graph on the right-hand side differs notably from the other two representations. We can assume that in the case of the right-hand graph, a bot network is present, because the referential behavior of the nodes (i.e. of individual Twitter accounts) is uncommon; it seems as if the users are making references to unusually high numbers of other users. Additionally, the referenced users in such a network are often those that have a great number of followers, e.g. celebrities. This strategy is most probably used to reach the greatest possible dispersion of a given content. It stands to reason that contents that are spread in this manner are highly likely to contain some form of misinformation. The analysis of the structures in a social network, therefore, not only reveals bots but can also point to instances of information campaigns. Thus, network analysis can support the identification of fake news as described in the previous paragraph.

5.4. Event Detection and Extraction

The information space can be considered as a source of information on the physical world. Within the information space, messages about actual and planned events are exchanged. These are to be extracted in order to enhance the situational awareness in the physical word.

We are currently carrying out work on an event detector. The aim of the event detector is to extract event information from a news stream and use this information to create entries in an event data base or to update existing event representations. An important challenge for an event detector is identity management: care must be taken to ascertain what different sources are actually reporting about. The question whether distinct events are under discussion or various messages rather report on the same event, albeit in different manners, has to be answered.

5.5. Sentiment Analysis

Sentiment analysis is a widely known approach in linguistics to determine an individual's attitude towards an entity, e.g., an object or an event. To achieve this, text written by an individual, may it be a long statement or merely a tweet about a given topic, is analysed with regard to its polarity. The content can then be classified as positive, negative or neutral. We did not yet integrate sentiment analysis into the dashboard prototype.

Sentiment analysis can be applied to the output of the other tools introduced in this chapter. Regarding language statistics, it can for example be examined in which contexts popular hashtags are used and how they are perceived by social media users.

Events that were detected in the information space are also of interest for sentiment analysis. We assume that by determining opinions towards events, specific interest groups can be identified. These groups can have opposing standpoints. Information about the forming and existence of these groups is relevant, as it may be that conflicts in the information space might also be carried out in the physical world.

Finally, sentiment analysis can reveal the attitudes towards institutions and organisations within the theatre of operations. This comes out as crucial in external missions like humanitarian missions or peace-keeping missions where the partners depend on cooperation with the local population.

6. Prototype

An information space dashboard is a management tool which comes with a collection of various components/apps for (i) accessing the information space, i.e. collecting data, (ii) analyzing data and (iii) visualizing analysis results. Data can be in diverse modalities, including texts in various languages, images, audio and video. At present, we only handle text data. Data analysis components should contribute to answering questions on what is happening, what is being reported (and what is not) and what will (supposedly) happen. Rather than giving an answer on one of these questions, the tools are to support the analyst in finding an answer. Visualization components serve both comprehensibility of analysis results and information exploration.

Figure 2: Dashboard Prototype

Figure 2 shows our prototype of an information space dashboard. In the preceding chapter, we have described worthwhile components, of which some have been fully implemented while others are still in a developmental state.

7. Demonstration Case

In the following, we will describe a demonstration case that deploys the above mentioned tools by reference to two self-compiled text corpora. Both corpora comprise reactions to the incident in Chemnitz, Germany at the 26th of August 2018, where a conflict at a city festival lead to the stabbing and in consequence death of one individual involved. Reports about the nationality and possible migrant status of the alleged attacker subsequently gave rise to a demonstration by right wing extremists that was accompanied by assaults against immigrants, the police and opposing demonstrators. In opposition to these developments, counter-activities took place, among them a concert against racism under the motto "Wir sind mehr" ("We are more") a few days later. The entire situation was complex and confusing. We assume that with reference to the information space a clearer overview and better situational awareness could have been reached.

In the demonstration case, we take the view of an operator who has to elicit what is happening at present, what is reported about recent events and what is likely to happen next. As she cannot solve this task manually, she falls back on automatized processes and applies the information space dashboard. The tools of the information space dashboard should be used to analyse live data. The present demonstration case, however, exploits historical data for the purpose of illustration.

7.1. Data

One of our corpora is a Twitter corpus, the other consists of articles by the German Press Agency (dpa), cf. Table 1.

Both corpora were compiled by using the keyword "Chemnitz" as a search term. The Twitter Corpus was compiled during the time of the incidents in Chemnitz. The dpa corpus includes articles from the whole year 2018; we focus only on the ones that are concerned with the mentioned events.

We use two distinct corpora because we assume that the situation can be grasped better if different sources are factored in. It can be supposed that the language of the Twitter Corpus is far more informal and displays subjective stances, while dpa releases are written in an objective and formal style. We deemed this to not be problematic but rather an accurate depiction of the domain in which an information space dashboard would be used.

Corpus	Tokens	Types
Twitter	9413464	170073
dpa	257637	28839

Table 1: Corpus Overview

7.2. Exemplary Application of Tools

The operator firstly has to define a starting point for her task. To quickly gain initial insights, the analysis of word frequencies – both from the texts and their metadata – is applied. During this analysis, stop words are ignored in order to focus only on the tokens that are semantically relevant.

At this point, the operator detects two hashtags on Twitter that are widespread. These are #wirsindmehr ("we are more") and #afd ("Alternative for Germany", a German far-right political party). While the meaning of the abbreviation "afd" is known, "wirsindmehr" needs further inspection. Therefore, the operator consults an additional data pool, namely dpa data. In several articles she finds that the hashtag #wirsindmehr is the motto of a free concert that takes a stand against racism (dpa, 2018). Due to the popularity of the hashtag, and consequently of the concert, she expects that the event will be well-attended.

To get a deeper understanding of the current mindset of the population, the operator turns back to Twitter and analyses tweets that include the hashtags #wirdsindmehr and #afd with regard to their sentiment/polarity. She selects data from social media as it conveys more subjectivity. She finds that while #wirsindmehr is supposed to stand for something positive, negative sentiments are connected to it, too. This can be seen as combinations of hashtags occur like, e.g., #wirsindmehr #ihrseiderbärmlich ("we are more you are pathetic"), #wirsindmehr #ihrseidscheiße ("we are more you are shit") and #ihrseidesnichtwert #wirsindmehr ("you are not worth it we are more"). The fact that the hashtag is used in a very positive and simultaneously an aggressive way is in indicator that (at least) two factions with greatly different opinions are forming in the population.

In a next step, the operator searches tweets about the concert that transfer negative sentiment to detect if users call for criminal acts or spread misinformation, both consciously or unconsciously, in order to substantiate their stance. A network analysis can reveal such behavior further and is applied subsequently.

The operator comes to the assessment that polarisation is rather increasing. Aggressive language lets violent incidents around the concert appear probable. Police forces are to be prepared accordingly.

8. Conclusions

We introduced the concept of an information space dashboard as a tool comprising components for data collection, data analysis and visualization. The aim of the dashboard is to support analysts in creating a common operation picture of the information space and, thus, contributing to overall situational awareness, including both the physical world and the information space. A first prototype including components for quantitative text analysis, text clustering and classification and network analysis has been created. Further components, namely for event detection and sentiment analysis, are under development. The information space dashboard is, thus, work in progress. As it will have to be adapted to changing tasks and conditions it will inherently be always work in progress: additional data source will have to be included and further analyses will have to be enabled.

Beside the development of additional components, next steps include evaluations with (potential) operators and other subject matter experts. User groups of diverse domains are to be considered: EU external civilian missions and UN missions are dependant on awareness of the situation in their theatres of operations. The same is true for the military which discusses information space operations in the context of defense against hybrid warfare. Of course, police forces have to be aware of activities in the information space – e.g., to be able to prevent hate crimes which are often announced in advance (Nagle, 2017) – but also emergency forces in order to get a better view on the situation and urgent needs, e.g., during disasters like floods or wild fires.

Observation and analysis of the information space can cause a bad taste as it is associatively linked with surveillance, censorship and suppression. Naturally, technology like an information space dashboard can be used for such ends. One means to prevent that is to make sure existing laws regarding privacy and freedom of speech are obeyed. The protection of individuals and their right to express themselves openly without fear of unwarranted consequences has a high priority, which means that not any arbitrary data source may be exploited. Furthermore, to avoid both misuse and the misunderstanding of actual, proper usage, it might be an adequate measure to make analytics transparent and provide a public overview on the information space. How this can be reached best, is still an open issue for us.

9. Bibliographical References

Bergh, A. (2019). Massage the message: Modularising software for influence operation detection in social media. In *Proceedings of the 24th International Command and Control Research Technology Symposium*, pages 1–14, Laurel, Maryland USA.

Boyd, J. (1975). The Essence of Winning and Loosing. https://www.danford.net/boyd/essence.htm.

Böttger, K. (2008). *Die häufigsten Fehler russischer Deutschlerner: Ein Handbuch für Lehrende*. Peter Lang Verlag, Münster.

Colbaugh, R. and Glass, K. (2012). Early warning analysis for social diffusion events. *Security Informatics*, 1(1):18.

dpa. (2018). Wie Chemnitz gegen sein Image als hässliche Stadt kämpft. https://www.suedkurier.de/ueberregional/politik/Wie-Chemnitz-gegen-sein-Image-als-haesslich e-Stadt-kaempft;art410924,9873202.

Franke, T. (2011). Social media: the frontline of cyberdefence? *NATO Review*.

Gladrow, W. (1998). *Russisch im Spiegel des Deutschen: Eine Einführung in den russisch-deutschen und deutsch-russischen Sprachvergleich*. Peter Lang Verlag, Frankfurt am Main.

Helbing, D., Brockmann, D., Chadefaux, T., Donnay, K., Blanke, U., Woolley-Meza, O., Moussaid, M., Johansson, A., Krause, J., Schutte, S., and Perc, M. (2014). How to Save Human Lives with Complexity Science. *European Journal for Security Research*, 4(1):51–71.

Kwak, H., Lee, C., Park, H., and Moon, S. (2010). What is Twitter, a social network or a news media? In *Proceedings of the 19th international conference on World wide web - WWW '10*, pages 11–13, New York, New York USA.

Lerman, K. and Hogg, T. (2012). Using stochastic models to describe and predict social dynamics of web users. *ACM Transactions on Intelligent Systems and Technologies*.

Leskovec, J. and Lang, K. (2008). Statistical properties of community structure in large social and information networks. *Proceedings of the 17th international conference on World Wide Web. ACM*, pages 695–704.

Li, M., Lin, Y., Hoover, J., Whitehead, S., Voss, C. R., Dehghani, M., and Ji, H. (2019). Multilingual Entity, Relation, Event and Human Value Extraction. In *Proceedings of the 2019 Conference of the North American Chapter of the Association for Computational Linguistics (Demonstrations)*, pages 110–115, Minneapolis, Minnesota USA.

Liu, H., Qin, W., and Wan, X. (2019). An Interactive Chinese News Synthesis System. In *Proceedings of the 2019 Conference of the North American Chapter of the Association for Computational Linguistics (Demonstrations)*, pages 18–23, Minneapolis, Minnesota USA.

Nadeem, M., Fang, W., Xu, B., Mohtarami, M., and Glass, J. (2019). FAKTA: An Automatic End-to-End Fact Checking System. In *Proceedings of the 2019 Conference of the North American Chapter of the Association for Computational Linguistics (Demonstrations)*, pages 78–83, Minneapolis, Minnesota USA.

Nagle, A. (2017). *Kill All Normies: Online Culture Wars from 4chan and Tumblr to Trump and the Alt-Right*. Zero Books.

Page, R. (2012). The linguistics of self-branding and micro-celebrity in twitter: The role of hashtags. *Discourse Communication*, 6(2):181–201.

Pritzkau, A. (2019). Vertrauenswürdiger Meinungsaustausch im Kontext von Polarisierung, Desinformation.

Qi, G.-J., Aggarwal, C. C., and Huang, T. (2012). Community detection with edge content in social media networks. In *Data Engineering (ICDE), 2012 IEEE 28th International Conference on. IEEE*, pages 534–545, Washington, DC USA.

Schade, U., Pritzkau, A., Claeser, D., Dembach, M., and Kent, S. (2018). "Fake News" und ihre Identifikation.

Schmitz, H.-C., Deneckere, M., de Zan, T., and Gräther, W. (2019). Situational Awareness, Information Exchange and operational Control for Civilian EU Missions. *European Journal for Security Research*, 4(1):51–71.

Woolley, S. and Howard, P. N., (2017). *Computational Propaganda Worldwide: Executive Summary*, pages 1–14. S.C. Woolley and Philip N. Howard, Oxford, UK.

Proceedings of the Workshop on Social Threats in Online Conversations: Understanding and Management (STOC-2020), pages 35–40
Language Resources and Evaluation Conference (LREC 2020), Marseille, 11–16 May 2020

Is this hotel review truthful or deceptive? A platform for disinformation detection through computational stylometry

Antonio Pascucci[1], Raffaele Manna[1], Ciro Caterino[2], Vincenzo Masucci[2], Johanna Monti[1]
L'Orientale University of Naples - UNIOR NLP Research Group[1], Expert System Corp.[2]
Via Duomo 219 Naples (Italy)[1], Via Nuova Poggioreale 60 Naples (Italy)[2]
{apascucci,rmanna,jmonti}@unior.it, {ccaterino,vmasucci}@expertsystem.com

Abstract

In this paper, we present a web service platform for disinformation detection in hotel reviews written in English. The platform relies on a hybrid approach of computational stylometry techniques, machine learning and linguistic rules written using COGITO©, Expert System Corp.'s semantic intelligence software thanks to which it is possible to analyze texts and extract all their characteristics. We carried out a research experiment on the *Deceptive Opinion Spam* corpus, a balanced corpus composed of 1,600 hotel reviews of 20 Chicago hotels split into four datasets: positive truthful, negative truthful, positive deceptive and negative deceptive reviews. We investigated four different classifiers and we detected that Simple Logistic is the most performing algorithm for this type of classification.

Keywords: Computational Stylometry, Disinformation Detection, Web Services.

1. Introduction

Disinformation is a phenomenon that is becoming part of everyday life. The phenomenon is uncontrollable, especially if we consider that social media and blogs are breeding grounds for news diffusion and that the higher the number of sharing of news, the more people are reached by the news. One of the fields in which disinformation is increasing quickly is hotel reviews, both for positive and for negative reviews. There may be an interest to spread positive or negative fake news about hotels. The main idea of our research is to reduce the impact of disinformation. For this reason, we developed a platform able answer to the question: is this hotel review truthful or deceptive? The paper is organized as follows: In Section 2 we present Related Work. In Section 3 we describe Computational Stylometry and some stylistic features and in Section 4 we present the *Deceptive Opinion Spam* corpus and we show the results of our testing. In Section 5 we propose the platform, ethical considerations are in Section 6 and Conclusions are in Section 7 along with Future Work.

2. Related Work

The proposed approach to detect disinformation in hotel reviews is certainly not the first one based on Computational Stylometry (CS) and Machine Learning (ML) / Deep Learning (DL) techniques. CS is presented in Section 4, DL exploits artificial neural networks with representation learning, while ML is the computer ability to learn from data. ML algorithms allow the system to preserve in its knowledge base each feature characteristic learned during the training process.
Despite "disinformation" and "fake news" represent two different concepts, they should be considered as close together, since they are both characterized by stylistic features typical of those who are lying. Disinformation is defined as *false information spread to deceive people*[1], while "fake news" *describes false stories that appear to be news, usually created to influence political views or as a joke*[2]. There is also a subtle difference between disinformation (incorrect information disseminated deliberately) and misinformation (that represents incorrect information disseminated unintentionally) (Egelhofer and Lecheler, 2019). (Kumar et al., 2016) investigated hoax articles presence on Wikipedia. The scholars used a large dataset of discovered hoaxes and detected that despite the community is efficient at identifying hoaxes, there is still a small number of these that survive for a long time. In their research, the scholars focused on the structure and content of the article and its mention in other articles. Their hoax/non-hoax classifier achieved an accuracy of 86% outperforming humans by a large margin (66%). In 2018, (Bakir and McStay, 2018) investigated the disinformation issue in the 2016 US presidential election campaign from an economic point of view. The scholars discovered a new version of disinformation, driven by profit and exploited by professional persuaders: it's about *emphatic media* (McStay, 2016), that represents personally and targeted news produced by *algo-journalism* (automated journalism), namely news articles generated by software through artificial intelligence.
As stated by (Lazer et al., 2018), addressing fake news requires a multidisciplinary effort. Despite authors of fake hotel reviews decide which words use, they can't handle the stylistic features that belong to the writing style and that make them unique. Considering that we detected stylistic features that characterize fake hotel review, we answer to (Lazer et al., 2018)'s request and we offer the potential of CS techniques in detecting fake hotel reviews. The "opinion spam" concept is very close to that of disinformation and mainly concerns in intentionally writing

[1] https://dictionary.cambridge.org/dictionary/english/disinformation
[2] https://dictionary.cambridge.org/dictionary/english/fake-news

fake reviews to products, restaurants or hotel (as in our case). The research of (Jindal and Liu, 2008) reveals that there are three different categories of opinion spam:

- untruthful opinions (undeserving positive reviews to some target objects to promote them or malicious negative reviews to some other objects to damage their reputation);
- reviews on brands only (those that do not comment on the specific product, but only the brand);
- non-reviews (those that are not reviews because contain advertisements)

(Ott et al., 2011) built a corpus composed of 400 truthful and 400 deceptive hotel reviews and proved that while n-grams based models are the best approach in identifying deceptive hotel reviews (89% of accuracy), a combination approach using psycholinguistically-motivated features (such as the number of words, lexical diversity, the score of narrativity) and n-grams features can perform slightly better (89.8% of accuracy). (Feng et al., 2012) exploit a Support Vector Machine (SVM) algorithm (Cortes and Vapnik, 1995) to build a classifier. The scholars used the corpus of (Ott et al., 2011) and two additional corpora and based their research on syntactical and lexical features and analyzed the text data with decision trees (DL approach) and achieved 91,2% of accuracy. The performances achieved by (Feng et al., 2012) improved those of (Ott et al., 2011), and demonstrated how a large use of personal pronouns (*I*) and possessive adjective (*my*) characterize deceptive hotel reviews.

(Popat et al., 2017) assessed the credibility of claims based on the occurrence of assertive and factive verbs, hedges, implicative words, report verbs and discourse markers. (Horne and Adali, 2017) focused on writing style and complexity to differentiate real news from fake news. The scholars used the number of occurrences of part-of-speech tags, swearing and slang words, stop words, punctuation, and negation as stylistic features. As stated by (Conroy et al., 2015), one of the best intuition in fake news and disinformation detection is that of (Feng et al., 2012): a deceptive writer with no experience with an event or object (e.g., never visited the hotel in question) may include contradictions or omission of facts present in profiles on similar topics.

3. Computational Stylometry

CS is a research area of Computational Linguistics that uses statistic techniques to analyze the literary style (Zheng et al., 2006). These techniques, through automatic linguistic analysis of texts, allow us to find countless personality traits. Wincenty Lutosławski (1863–1954), the one who coined the term *stylometry*, compared the style to handwriting: "If handwriting can be so exactly determined as to afford certainty as to its identity, so also with style, since style is more personal and characteristic than handwriting" (Lutosławski, 1897).

We have to consider that despite a deceptive review is written with greater intention to label it as positive or negative, stylistic features are not intentional but unintentional and result from sociological factors (such as age, gender and education level) and psychological factors (that include personality, mental health and being a native speaker or not) (Daelemans, 2013). It means that authors of deceptive review can certainly decide which words use in their review, but it is equally true that they can't handle the stylistic features that belong to their writing style. We believe that deceptive texts contain specific stylistic features that differentiate them from those truthful.

3.1. Stylistic Features

Almost all approaches in detecting disinformation and opinion spam focus on bag-of-words and part-of-speech models. As argued by (Ren and Ji, 2019) also linguistic (the functional aspect of a text), psychological (social, emotional and cognitive aspects), personal (any references to work, religion, etc.) and spoken (fillers and agreement words) features have to be taken into account. Several stylistic features characterize writing style and distinguish two or more different styles. Here we report a short list of stylistic features: sentence length (Argamon et al., 2003), word length distributions (Zheng et al., 2006), punctuation (Baayen et al., 1996), use of function words (Mosteller and Wallace, 1963), vocabulary richness (De Vel et al., 2001), use of a specific class of verbs or adjectives, use of first/third person.

Concerning CS, it is important to stress that stylometric analysis must focus only on unintentional choices by the writer of a text. Here we list some of the features that characterise deceptive texts in the corpus we investigated: high use of adverbs, high use of common nouns, high use of inappropriate lowercase on characters, high use of may/might and intensifiers, low use of punctuation, lower readability index, rare use of foreign terms, and high use of to + infinitive.

4. Corpus Analysis

We investigated the *Deceptive Opinion Spam* corpus in order to use it as pilot for the platform. The corpus consists of truthful and deceptive hotel reviews of 20 Chicago hotels and contains 400 truthful positive reviews from *TripAdvisor* and 400 deceptive positive reviews from *Mechanical Turk* described in (Ott et al., 2011) in addition to 400 truthful negative reviews from *Expedia, Hotels.com, Orbitz, Priceline, TripAdvisor* and *Yelp* and 400 deceptive negative reviews from *Mechanical Turk* described in (Ott et al., 2013). Each dataset consists of 20 reviews for each of the 20 most popular Chicago hotels.

4.1. Workflow

Our workflow for stylistic features extraction consists in the following steps:

- I) *Linguistic Definition of Stylometric Features*: since each author operates grammatical choices when writing a text, we organize all the grammatical characteristics of the texts under study in a taxonomy to detect the authorial fingerprint based on the grammatical choices done. This first step is carried out thanks to COGITO©, that allows us to write LR and to perform word-sense disambiguation;

- II) *Semantic Engine Development*: we train the semantic engine to extract the features from the analyzed texts. The semantic engine is implemented thanks to COGITO©'s semantic network (*Sensigrafo*) - that can operate word-sense disambiguation - with the addition of the rules we built;

- III) *Training Set Analysis*: the training set is analysed and all features (based on the grammatical choices done by the writer) are extracted;

- IV) *ML*: In the last step, we exploit the features extracted to train the model to detect these features in the dataset. ML process is carried out exploiting WEKA platform (Hall et al., 2009) (a software with machine learning tools and algorithms for data analysis) and we build each classifier with the support of one of the algorithms available in WEKA.

4.2. Test

We built four classifiers trained with four different algorithms: Simple Logistic (SLO), Logistic (LOG), Sequential Minimal Optimization (SMO), and Random Forest (RFO). As we have mentioned, the whole corpus is composed of 1,600 reviews.
We decided to test all the aforementioned algorithms using the 10-folds cross-validation method. In Table 1 we show the 10-folds cross-validation results.

	SLO	LOG	SMO	RFO
10-f. cross-validation	**0,742**	0,721	0,738	0,702

Table 1: Percentage of correctly classified instances

Then, in order to evaluate the real performances of all the classifiers, we split the data into two sets: a training set composed of 1,200 of the 1,600 reviews and a test set composed of the remaining 400 reviews (200 truthful reviews and 200 deceptive randomly selected). In Table 2 we show the results of the test set.
According to Table 2 and to the confusion matrices in Figures 1, 2, 3, and 4, Simple Logistic is the best performing algorithm for this type of experiment and we decided to use it for our platform.

	SLO	LOG	SMO	RFO
Test experiment	**0,755**	0,707	0,725	0,710

Table 2: Percentage of correctly classified instances

The results we achieved (77.5%) do not improve those of (Ott et al., 2011) (89%) and those of (Feng et al., 2012) (89.9%). The reason is in the approach we adopted, that mainly focus on linguistic features and does not consider features (such as n-grams) that proved to be very useful in building deceptive detection models.

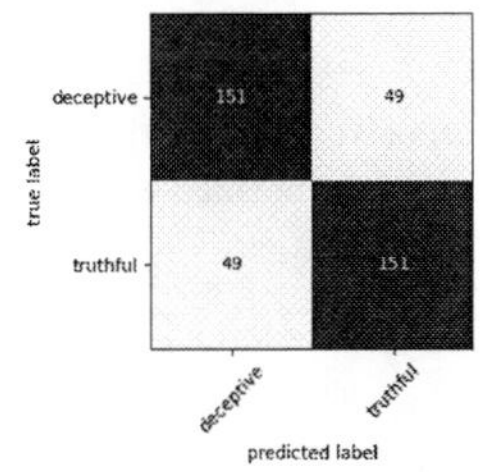

Figure 1: Confusion matrix of Simple Logistic classifier

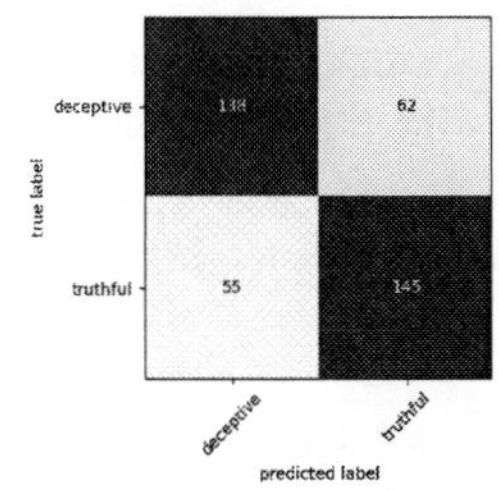

Figure 2: Confusion matrix of Logistic classifier

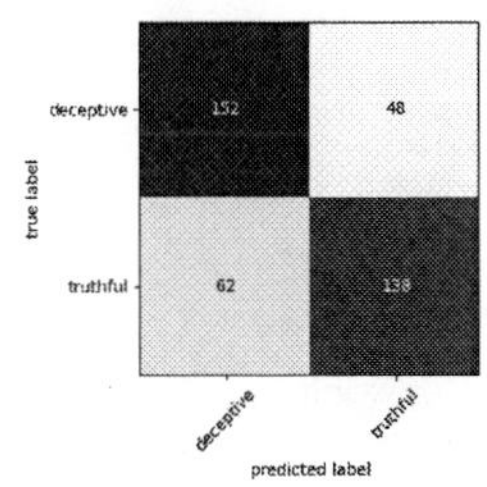

Figure 3: Confusion matrix of Sequential Minimal Optimization classifier

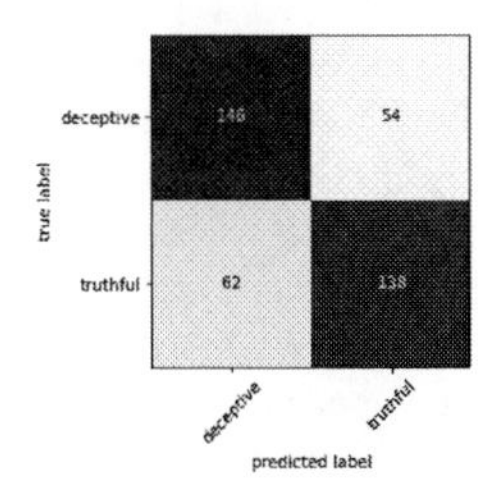

Figure 4: Confusion matrix of Random Forest classifier

5. Web service platform

The deceptive classification is provided through a REST web service which accepts as body input the text to classify.

The logic of the system consists of three main functional blocks:

- I) **Document Repository** - any document submitted to the system can be memorized together with a set of metadata about the document;
- II) **Computational Stylometry** - any document has to undergo a process of stylometric analysis. Thanks to our semantic intelligence software we can extract all stylistic features. The output is a set of stylometric features that are added to the document metadata (this block represents the whole workflow we have shown in Section 4.2, with the exception of ML process that is part of the third block);
- III) **Traits Prediction** - traits prediction refers to the profiling task thanks to ML techniques.

In Figure 5 we show the process. The method is POST, namely a method that accepts a text in the body and returns a JSON.

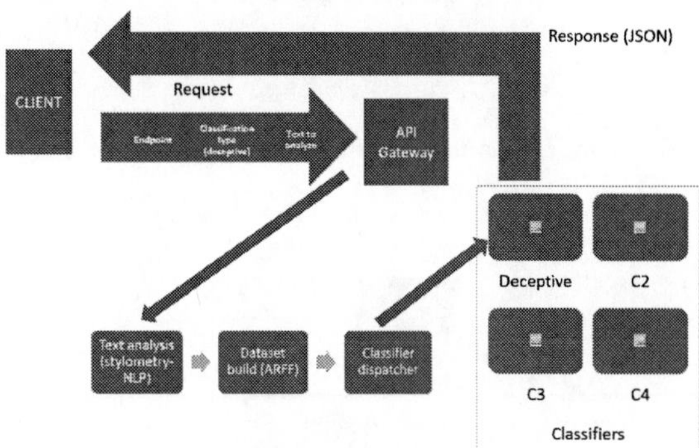

Figure 5: Web service platform process

The endpoint path contains information about the required type of classification, in this case, the *deceptive* one, so at the beginning, the user asks for a deceptive type of classification (it means the type of classification that the user needs and this type of classification includes two classes: *truthful* and *deceptive*) on the text the user provides. The API Gateway is in charge to receive requests and to begin the analysis process. The first step is the text analysis performed by the NLP technology, in order to extract stylometric features that will be used to classify the document in question. The second step is the ML process. For this process, we rely on WEKA platform (Hall et al., 2009), which requires a special file (ARFF) that contains all the information related to the text (namely the input text and the stylometric features extracted). The ARFF file is the input for the classifier, invocated from our classifier dispatcher module. Classification results are formatted in JSON and sent to the requester (CLIENT). Here we report an example of classification done on a text that belongs to the corpus:

Text:
After recent work stay at the Affinia Hotel, I can definitely say I will be coming back. They offer so many in room amenities and services, just a very comfortable and relaxed place to be. My most enjoyable experience at the Affinia Hotel was the amazing customization they offered, I would recommend Affinia hotel to anyone looking for a nice place to stay.

Prediction:
"actual": null,
"distribution":[0.7724841302455, 0.22751586975446],
"predicted": "deceptive",
"probability": 0.7724841302455,
"doc_name": "hotelopinion578-test"

The example reported above confirms that deceptive reviews are characterized by the use of intensifiers (*definitely, so many, a very, most enjoyable*). The review also lacks details, with reference only to general characteristics. Another characteristic that belongs to deceptive reviews is the repetition of the hotel name.
On these bases, our platform accepts hotel reviews written in English and returns to the user a prediction on the reliability of the review. It is important to stress, as shown in the example above, that the user receives a JSON that contains also a degree of probability of the prediction. Given the results of the test carried out on the *Deceptive Opinion Spam* we believe that our platform could make an important contribution to disinformation detection.

6. Ethical Considerations

The ethical argument has fundamental importance, especially if it is about public data closely linked to people. In fact, when we talk about author profiling and authorship attribution (two important branches of CS), we immediately think about the effects of our prediction. Then, privacy is the most important issue when we deal with profiling. In a case like this, we just need texts. All the other information (name of the authors, their age, thier origin and so on) are unnecessary. It means that possible negative impacts of our technology (the disinformation detection platform) are strongly mitigated. In other words, in the case of disinformation detection, it is not essential to know who wrote the review, and anonymization of reviews can mitigate ethical issues that may arise when these type of technologies are available to everyone.

7. Conclusions and Future Work

In this paper we have shown an experiment carried out on the *Deceptive Opinion Spam* Corpus, a corpus composed of 1,600 hotel reviews of 20 Chicago hotels split into four datasets: positive truthful, negative truthful, positive deceptive and negative deceptive reviews. The test has shown that the most performing algorithm is Simple Logistic, that correctly classified 75,5% of the test set we used. On the basis of these results, we developed a disinformation detection platform for hotel reviews written in English, in order to allow the user to submit a review and detect if it is deceptive or truthful and the percentage of probability of the prediction. It is not excluded that we will provide versions for other languages too. In this paper, we have shown how a linguistic-rule based approach can help detect deceptive hotel reviews with good results. As a next step of our research we also aim to investigate more innovative techniques such as the use of neural networks and unsupervised learning approaches and to compare it with our current approach.

8. Acknowledgements

This research has been partly supported by the PON Ricerca e Innovazione 2014-20 and the POR Campania FSE 2014-2020 funds. Authorship contribution is as follows: Antonio Pascucci is author of Sections 1, 2, 3, 4, and 5. Sections 6 and 7 are in common between Antonio Pascucci and Raffaele Manna. This research has been developed in the framework of two Innovative Industrial PhD projects in Computational Stylometry (CS) by "L'Orientale" University of Naples in cooperation with Expert System Corp. We sincerely thank Ciro Caterino for helping us in developing the web service platform. We are also grateful to Vincenzo Masucci and Expert System Corp. for providing COGITO©for research and to Prof. Johanna Monti for supervising the research.

9. Bibliographical References

Argamon, S., Šarić, M., and Stein, S. S. (2003). Style mining of electronic messages for multiple authorship discrimination: first results. In *Proceedings of the ninth ACM SIGKDD international conference on Knowledge discovery and data mining*, pages 475–480. ACM.

Baayen, H., Van Halteren, H., and Tweedie, F. (1996). Outside the cave of shadows: Using syntactic annotation to enhance authorship attribution. *Literary and Linguistic Computing*, 11(3):121–132.

Bakir, V. and McStay, A. (2018). Fake news and the economy of emotions: Problems, causes, solutions. *Digital journalism*, 6(2):154–175.

Conroy, N. J., Rubin, V. L., and Chen, Y. (2015). Automatic deception detection: Methods for finding fake news. *Proceedings of the Association for Information Science and Technology*, 52(1):1–4.

Cortes, C. and Vapnik, V. (1995). Support-vector networks. *Machine learning*, 20(3):273–297.

Daelemans, W. (2013). Explanation in computational stylometry. In *International Conference on Intelligent Text Processing and Computational Linguistics*, pages 451–462. Springer.

De Vel, O., Anderson, A., Corney, M., and Mohay, G. (2001). Mining e-mail content for author identification forensics. *ACM Sigmod Record*, 30(4):55–64.

Egelhofer, J. L. and Lecheler, S. (2019). Fake news as a two-dimensional phenomenon: a framework and research agenda. *Annals of the International Communication Association*, 43(2):97–116.

Feng, S., Banerjee, R., and Choi, Y. (2012). Syntactic stylometry for deception detection. In *Proceedings of the 50th Annual Meeting of the Association for Computational Linguistics: Short Papers-Volume 2*, pages 171–175. Association for Computational Linguistics.

Hall, M., Frank, E., Holmes, G., Pfahringer, B., Reutemann, P., and Witten, I. H. (2009). The weka data mining software: an update. *ACM SIGKDD explorations newsletter*, 11(1):10–18.

Horne, B. D. and Adali, S. (2017). This just in: fake news packs a lot in title, uses simpler, repetitive content in text body, more similar to satire than real news. In *Eleventh International AAAI Conference on Web and Social Media*.

Jindal, N. and Liu, B. (2008). Opinion spam and analysis. In *Proceedings of the 2008 international conference on web search and data mining*, pages 219–230.

Kumar, S., West, R., and Leskovec, J. (2016). Disinformation on the web: Impact, characteristics, and detection of wikipedia hoaxes. In *Proceedings of the 25th international conference on World Wide Web*, pages 591–602.

Lazer, D. M., Baum, M. A., Benkler, Y., Berinsky, A. J., Greenhill, K. M., Menczer, F., Metzger, M. J., Nyhan, B., Pennycook, G., Rothschild, D., et al. (2018). The science of fake news. *Science*, 359(6380):1094–1096.

Lutosławski, W. (1897). *The origin and growth of Plato's logic: with an account of Plato's style and of the chronology of his writings*. Longmans, Green and Company.

McStay, A. (2016). Empathic media: The rise of emotion ai. *Arts & Humanities Research Council*.

Mosteller, F. and Wallace, D. L. (1963). Inference in an authorship problem: A comparative study of discrimination methods applied to the authorship of the disputed federalist papers. *Journal of the American Statistical Association*, 58(302):275–309.

Ott, M., Choi, Y., Cardie, C., and Hancock, J. T. (2011). Finding deceptive opinion spam by any stretch of the imagination. In *Proceedings of the 49th annual meeting of the association for computational linguistics: Human language technologies-volume 1*, pages 309–319. Association for Computational Linguistics.

Popat, K., Mukherjee, S., Strötgen, J., and Weikum, G. (2017). Where the truth lies: Explaining the credibility of emerging claims on the web and social media. In *Proceedings of the 26th International Conference on World Wide Web Companion*, pages 1003–1012.

Ren, Y. and Ji, D. (2019). Learning to detect deceptive opinion spam: A survey. *IEEE Access*, 7:42934–42945.

Zheng, R., Li, J., Chen, H., and Huang, Z. (2006). A framework for authorship identification of online messages: Writing-style features and classification techniques. *Journal of the American society for information science and technology*, 57(3):378–393.

10. Language Resource References

Ott, M., Choi, Y., Cardie, C., and Hancock, J. T. (2011). Finding deceptive opinion spam by any stretch of the imagination. In *Proceedings of the 49th annual meeting of the association for computational linguistics: Human language technologies-volume 1*, pages 309–319. Association for Computational Linguistics.

Ott, M., Cardie, C., and Hancock, J. T. (2013). Negative deceptive opinion spam. In *Proceedings of the 2013 conference of the north american chapter of the association for computational linguistics: human language technologies*, pages 497–501.

Proceedings of the Workshop on Social Threats in Online Conversations: Understanding and Management (STOC-2020), pages 41–47
Language Resources and Evaluation Conference (LREC 2020), Marseille, 11–16 May 2020

Corpus Development for Studying Online Disinformation Campaign: A Narrative + Stance Approach

Mack Blackburn, Ning Yu,
John Berrie, Brian Gordon, David Longfellow, William Tirrell, Mark Williams
Leidos Inc.
4001 Fairfax Dr. Arlington, VA 22203
{ mack.blackburn, ning.yu, john.w.berrie, brian.a.gordon, david.a.longfellow, william.c.tirrell, mark.b.williams}@abc.org

Abstract

Disinformation on social media is impacting our personal life and society. The outbreak of the new coronavirus is the most recent example for which a wealth of disinformation provoked fear, hate, and even social panic. While there are emerging interests in studying how disinformation campaigns form, spread, and influence target audiences, developing disinformation campaign corpora is challenging given the high volume, fast evolution, and wide variation of messages associated with each campaign. Disinformation cannot always be captured by simple factchecking, which makes it even more challenging to validate and create ground truth. This paper presents our approach to develop a corpus for studying disinformation campaigns targeting the White Helmets of Syria. We bypass directly classifying a piece of information as disinformation or not. Instead, we label the narrative and stance of tweets and YouTube comments about White Helmets. Narratives is defined as a recurring statement that is used to express a point of view. Stance is a high-level point of view on a topic. We demonstrate that narrative and stance together can provide a dynamic method for real world users, e.g., intelligence analysts, to quickly identify and counter disinformation campaigns based on their knowledge at the time.

Keywords: disinformation, narrative extraction, corpus development

1. Introduction

In this paper, we present our strategies for data collection and annotation to support studies of online disinformation spread within and across information platforms, mainly using a use case of disinformation campaigns towards the Syrian Civil Defense Force (a.k.a., White Helmets) on Twitter and YouTube. The biggest challenge in constructing such a corpus is how to annotate disinformation. Disinformation is not always easy to fact check; sometimes it can be a piece of true information used in a misleading context, or a fact that was once true but is now false. We propose to bypass directly labeling a piece of information as disinformation or not, instead labelling the narrative and stance of social media content about the White Helmets. In our context, *Narrative* is defined as a recurring statement that is used to express a point of view on a particular topic. Narratives may be explanations of events, interpretations of the motives of actors, statements which emphasize specific concepts, or other techniques to express a point of view. *Stance* is a point of view on a topic. These points of view should be very high level and should represent a user's attitude (usually for or against) a topic. While stance is the point of view itself, a narrative is a particular idea or claim which supports the stance. We show that narrative and stance together can provide a dynamic method for real world users, e.g., intelligence analysts, to quickly create their own data collection on disinformation campaigns with their context-specific knowledge. We first explain how we developed an on-topic corpus containing tweets, YouTube comments, and supporting data sources, then we discuss our initial efforts and lessons learned in defining, detecting and labeling narratives against a subset of this data. We developed an approach to extract individual narrative elements in a clearly interpretable form, drawing on work from information extraction and computational narratology. We also incorporated technologies such as semantic vector clustering in order to combine narrative elements with different structure but similar meaning. Finally, we briefly explain our ongoing efforts to refine and improve narrative and stance annotation guidelines.

2. Background

2.1 White Helmets disinformation campaign

Russia, in coordination with its allies, has orchestrated a large-scale online misinformation/disinformation campaign to discredit the White Helmets of Syria, who are potential witnesses to war crimes committed by the Assad Regime. Russia uses online social platforms like Twitter and YouTube to undermine the credibility and neutrality of the White Helmets by developing narratives about their association with terrorism (i.e., ISIS), Western governments, and even the black market organ trade. Studying such online disinformation operations may help forecast the impact of future disinformation campaigns and potentially allow early development of counter-message strategies.

2.2 Narrative

Narrative plays an important role in both online and offline environments and has been studied in the fields of literature, communication, marketing, and more recently, computational social science (e.g., Chambers and Jurafsky, 2008; Huhn 2019; Yarlott and Finlayson, 2016). Finlayson and Corman (2013) coined two levels of narratives. Level I narrative is related to event discourse: "a report of a sequence of actions or events that are locally coherent and connected, with clear chains of cause and effect concerning a set of agents and their goals and motivations." Most computational work on narrative focuses on Level I, and so does our narrative annotation. Level II narrative is related to action discourse and follows comprehensive narrative structure that adds things narratologists are concerned with such as use of metaphors and cultural tropes. This is an area of interest for future research.

Chambers and Jurafsky (2008) made early attempts to automatically extract, associate, and order narrative event chains from news articles. They parsed the raw text to extract narrative events tuples about a central actor. For each document, verb pairs linked by common entities are narrative events that make up a narrative chain, and each story can contain multiple narrative chains. Chambers and Jurafsky also ordered and clustered events in the same narrative chain. Miller (2018) discussed computational approaches, e.g., event extraction, to narrative detection. Our approach is closest to these computational narrative analyses.

Past research has often been conducted using lengthy documents such as news articles. There are fewer studies of narratives in the microblog space, where narratives can be generated by groups of users via communication with short messages and/or multi-media. The latter format is sometimes called "small stories" (Georgakopoulou, 2014). Stories created in this way may be contained entirely within one tweet, collaboratively constructed by multiple participants, or sequentially created by a single user across multiple tweets (Dayter, 2015; Georgakopoulou, 2014, 2016). Our work aims to extract elements of narratives and the narratives themselves from tweets and YouTube comments.

3. Data collection

3.1 Keyword Driven Data Gathering

Working with subject matter experts in information operation, we first created a list of keywords (e.g., "syria civil defense"), Hashtags (e.g., "#SyriaHoax") and Twitter accounts (e.g., @RT) that are related to online discussions of the White Helmets and/or from disinformation sources, in both English and Arabic. Querying this list through Gnip Historical PowerTrack API[1] against the period of April 2018 to April 2019 returns a total of 1.2 million tweets. The same keywords were also used to query YouTube Search API[2] and gathered information of 1,461 related YouTube videos and 631 channels. We downloaded basic video information such as title, as well as statistics composed of view, likes, dislikes, favorite and comment counts, comments, replies, and captions. To facilitate research of cross-platform information spread, we also get all tweets that refers to YouTube videos.

One drawback of keyword-based data gathering are the false positives due to use of keywords in a context different from the target one. For example, occasionally, White Helmets may be used in a sports context. We took a semi-automatic approach to address this challenge. On one hand, in search queries we reinforce the correct context word and add negative rules for known false context words, e.g., -(scooter OR bike OR bicycle OR football); on the other, we run topic modeling to identify clusters of false positive messages.

3.2 Privacy Protection

We identify personally identifiable information fields in our data (e.g., user ids, emails) and either remove or anonymize such information. Both our data gathering and anonymization strategies have been approved by our corporate security office and, in some cases, by online service providers (e.g., Twitter). For example, mentioning of a twitter user name in a Tweet "RT @SyriaCivilDef" will be anonymized as "RT @ iAo-MokhyIPkTNyhXbuJmQ."

While protecting personal privacy, we also try not to void data of analytic value by enabling researchers to link anonymized information. For example, URLs are anonymized by sections to allow matching at different levels: youtube.com/anonymizedA/anonymizedB will still partially match youtube.com/anonymizedA/anonymizedC while this similarity will vanish if URLs are anonymized as one single string.

3.3 Data Enrichment

We extend the data fields returned by data APIs to include information that may facilitate understanding of disinformation spread. Some enrichment examples are as follows.

Named entities are extracted using tools developed specifically for Twitter data (Ritter, 2011). It can help researchers focus on the mention of particular type of entity, e.g., location or person.

Segmented hashtags are hashtags separated into individual words, e.g., #SupportWH to "Support" and "WH" (Maddela, Xu, & Preotiuc, 2019). Hashtags are important in spreading information and in carrying crucial information across social networking and microblog platforms. Segmenting and analyzing hashtags reveal information contained in each and thus enable accurate hashtag alignment.

Sentiment is labeled at the message level using TweetMotif[3], which provides means for researchers to investigate the impact of sentiment on information spread.

User alignment provides a probability score in terms of how likely two accounts on different platforms belong to the same person. At this point, this is simply calculated by the string similarity of username (before they are anonymized) using the Levenshtein distance. This enrichment enables researchers to not only track information across platform, but also across multiple usernames belonging to the same user.

External references are pages linked from tweets. They either complete the information in the tweet or provide context for the tweet.

For Arabic messages, we also provide English translations using Google translate. For the rest of the paper focusing on narrative labelling, we are going to consider English data only as it is easier to interpret the results than Arabic data when it comes to narrative labeling.

4. Narrative Labelling

In our White Helmets data there are many narratives related to White Helmets, e.g., they are related to terrorist groups,

[1]https://developer.twitter.com/en/docs/tweets/batch-historical/overview

[2]https://developers.google.com/youtube/v3/docs/search/list

[3]https://github.com/ntietz/tweetment

they staged an attack at a particular location, or that they are saving lives. Many of them are not easily verified. Others rely on misleading information, have logical leaps, or are purely statements of opinion. Although researchers may rely on information sources as one factor to judge if a piece of information is disinformation or not, we cannot simply assume certain information sources will always spread disinformation about White Helmets because even propaganda sites share a mix of true and false information. Practically, we cannot manually label millions of messages either. In the rest of this section, we will present our data exploration with LDA to gain a sense of the topic space, then present alternative approaches to test to what extent automatic approaches can help us with narrative labeling.

4.1 Data Exploration with LDA

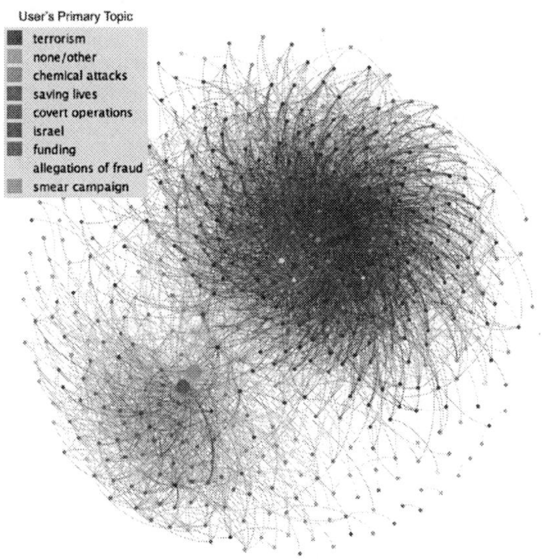

Figure 1: Retweet and quote network for the top users ranked by PageRank. Users are colored by the predominant keyword group in their tweets.

We ran LDA topic modeling (Blei, Ng, & Jordan 2003) on our data and expected to use topics to approximate narratives. However, sometimes LDA topics are less coherent, combine multiple distinct elements, or represent a semantic unit that cannot be interpreted as a narrative. For example, one LDA topic is represented by the words: *russia*, *assad*, *russian*, *regime*, *disinformation*, *claims*, *kremlin*, *target*, *crimes*, and *conspiracy*. This topic is useful in that it provides some insights on distributionally related content in the dataset. However, it would be a mistake to assume that all texts assigned high confidence for this topic share the same narrative. For example, below are two tweets that are assigned high confidence for this topic:

- "The White Helmets are eyewitnesses 193 to war crimes carried out by the Assad regime (which is backed by Russia)..."
- "How Twitter #disinformation is spread by a combination of Assad apologists, Kremlin bots, dupes and paid propagandists"

Although both tweets mention Assad and Russia aligned keywords, they have a distinctly different meaning.

To clean up the LDA results, we hand-selected narrative related keywords from both LDA output and common terms used in top tweets for each topic. Then we manually grouped these keywords into semantically similar sets. As a result, we got 57 sets (narratives). When mapping such keyword sets onto a retweet network of the most influential users, Figure 1 shows a visibly polarized network where users on each side talk about similar narratives, whether supporting or opposing the White Helmets. This suggests that there are possible disinformation campaigns (upper right) and counter campaigns (lower left) visible in our data.

Overall, several patterns became evident during exploration of the dataset: 1) Many authors and sources can collaboratively construct a narrative that is distributed across disconnected texts; 2) The bias or stance of the narrative toward some issue or entity is often the most important component. As a matter of fact, Lehnert (1981) stated that emotional states are the building blocks for a narrative text; and 3) A narrative can often be summarized with a single statement of fact or opinion, e.g., "rescuers."

4.2 Narrative Extraction Experiment

Next, we developed several narrative extraction methods, ran them against a 50,000 tweets subset of the White Helmets dataset, and tested them against the 500 most retweeted tweets manually annotated with one of the 57 narratives identified as described in section 4.1 (See Appendix A).

4.2.1 Model Selection

While event extraction systems such as McClosky et al., 2011; Reschke, et al., 2014; and Wang, 2018 may be effective at extracting narrative events, one additional consideration is that understanding of a narrative requires extracting elements which cannot be classified as an event in the sense of a change of state. For example, relationships between characters, or attributes assigned to characters in a story may be essential to understanding the narrative as intended. However, these kinds of narrative elements may be extracted using methods from open information extraction (OpenIE).

OpenIE systems are designed to extract relations between noun phrases (Mausam, 2016). Many OpenIE systems use a combination of dependency parsing and learned patterns (Mausam and Etzioni, 2012; Wu and Weld, 2010). While some IE systems only extract binary relations, expressions in natural language may also involve more than two noun phrases, or exactly one. Some OpenIE systems have already explored n-ary relations (Christensen and Etzioni, 2011; Pal and Mausam, 2016). Others have also utilized clustering of both noun phrases and relations in order to reduce semantic redundancy (Vashishth and Talukdar, 2018). We incorporate ideas from OpenIE into our verb phrase clustering algorithm, most notably n-ary relations and clustering of embeddings.

Verb Phrase Clustering (VerbPC): vectors are generated for each of the unique verb phrases extracted using dependency parsing, and those are clustered into 100 groups using agglomerative clustering. The number of clusters was fixed at 100 in order to have a fair comparison with LDA and NMF, which also had 100 clusters. An example of an extracted verb phrase: {'verb': ['stage'], 'nsubjpass': ['chemical', 'attack'], 'agent': ['militant']} for "Chemical attack staged by militants."

Ngram Clustering (NgramC1, NgramC2): Scikit-Learn is used to extract 1-3grams from all texts. The FastText vectors of each ngram are clustered using agglomerative clustering. We evaluated with two separate versions of this model: 1) number of clusters fixed at 100 (NgramC2), and 2) distance parameter of agglomerative clustering was set at 1.5 and the number of clusters was induced (NgramC1).

For comparison, we also tested the topic modeling algorithms **LDA** and **NMF** (non-negative matrix factorization) with tf/idf using 100 clusters. For both methods, each text is represented by a binary vector showing the topic with the highest confidence. Additionally, we used the naive approach of bag of words (**BoW**) vectors, limited to the top 500 most common 1-3 grams.

To evaluate each model, the output was fed to a K Nearest Neighbors classifier, and their precision and F1 were recorded in Table 1.

Method	F1	Precision
NgramC1	0.33	**0.71**
NgramC2	0.35	0.66
VerbPC	0.35	0.60
	Baselines	
BoW	0.28	0.60
LDA	0.36	0.57
NMF	0.38	0.64

Table 1: KNN Classification Results on Narrative Extraction Methods

4.2.2 Results and Discussions

The most precise algorithm is clustering of ngrams. Verb phrase clustering was more effective than LDA and BoW, but was less effective than NMF and ngram clustering. This may suggest that one approach forward would be to extract text units from the documents that are smaller and more common across texts than verb phrases, but would still convey more of a coherent meaning than ngrams alone. Phrase mining systems such as (Liu et al., 2015), which can extract high-quality readable phrases, may be effective here. While all embedding algorithms here used FastText and cosine distance for agglomerative clustering, incorporating more sophisticated semantic distance measurements may be more effective in the future.

4.3 Supervised Approach

Given that none of the fully automatic narrative extraction approaches we examined in section 4.2 yield results that are good enough to be used as ground truth and there is still more research to be done on this topic. Hence, we are pursuing in parallel a supervised learning approach, which requires more training data.

Here are the steps we plan to take to create the annotation set. Starting with the full data:

Twitter:

- Remove all texts that have fewer than 200 retweets
- Sample of unique texts randomly, weighted by # of times occurring in corpus, random ordering
- Final annotation set is 10,000 tweets

YouTube:

- Randomly Sample of unique texts, weighted by # of times occurring in corpus, with random ordering
- In the annotation set, the number of texts from YouTube should be proportional to the number of relevant YouTube texts in all unique text values.
- Final annotation set is length 10,000 * ((number of YouTube texts matching relevance query)/(number of unique texts))

After generating the annotation candidates, we asked 9 annotators for two annotation tasks: stance and narrative. We assigned a few small batches (30-60 pieces of text) to all annotators in order to see their agreement scores and make changes to the annotation guidelines if necessary. Once all annotators had completed 120 messages, we split the rest of the data into separate batches. Each annotator annotated 100 messages by themselves and then 100 together. Periodically we calculated the inter-annotator reliability by Fleiss' kappa to determine if we need to give them more guidance or modify the guidelines.

Once we have all the training data annotated, it will be used to train several supervised multi-classification systems with text representations from simple tf/idf vector to multilingual BERT or FastText with pretrained Spanish embeddings.

5. Conclusion and Future Work

In this paper, we have demonstrated our end-to-end effort in developing a corpus for studying disinformation campaigns across platforms. We focused on the most challenging annotation tasks and discussed our early exploration of an automatic approach to extract elements of narratives on microblogs. While our approach shows promising results, we still have a long way to go in terms of accurately generating ground truth data. Our future plans are two-fold: First, we will continue our focus on optimizing narrative event extraction as well as linking these events into narratives by taking full advantage of microblog attributes. Secondly, we will continue to improve our annotation guidelines and processes and start to explore a supervised approach.

6. Ethical Considerations

There are some privacy concerns related to the work we discussed here: disclosing social media users' personal point of view without their explicit consent (Fiesler and Proferes, 2018), and the risk of wrongly associating users with disinformation spread activities during our manual or automatic labeling process. To mitigate those risks, we anonymize our data, reach agreement with each social company regarding out data collection and anonymization plan, and strictly follow IRB and private guidance provided by the research program. We also only allow researchers who have completed DARPA privacy training and meet all privacy compliance requirements to access data.

7. Acknowledgements

We thank our anonymous reviewers for their valuable feedback. This material is based upon work supported by the Defense Advanced Research Projects Agency (DARPA) and the Army Research Office (ARO) under Contract No. W911NF-17-C-0095. The content of the information in this document does not necessarily reflect the position or the policy of the U.S. Government, and no official endorsement should be inferred.

8. Bibliographical References

Blei, D. M., Ng, A. Y., & Jordan, M. I. (2003). Latent dirichlet allocation. Journal of machine Learning research, 3(Jan), pp. 993-1022.

Chambers, N., & Jurafsky, D. (2008). Unsupervised learning of narrative event chains. In Proceedings of ACL-08: HLT. Association for Computational Linguistics, pp. 789–797.

Christensen, J., Soderland, S., & Etzioni, O. (2011). An analysis of open information extraction based on semantic role labeling. In Proceedings of the Sixth International Conference on Knowledge Capture, pp. 113-120.

Dayter, D. (2015). Small stories and extended narratives on twitter. Discourse, Context and Media, 10, pp. 19–26.

Fiesler, C., & Proferes, N. (2018). "Participant" perceptions of twitter research ethics. SocialMedia+ Society, 4(1):2056305118763366

Finlayson, M. A., & Corman, S. R. (2013). The military interest in narrative. Sprache und Datenverarbeitung, 37(1-2), pp. 173-191.

Georgakopoulou, A. (2014). Between narrative analysis and narrative inquiry: The long story of small stories research. Urban Language and Literacies, 131, pp. 1-17.

Hühn, P., et al. (eds.): The living handbook of narratology. Hamburg: Hamburg University. http://www.lhn.uni-hamburg.de/

Pal, H., & Mausam (2016). Demonyms and compound relational nouns in nominal open IE. In Proceedings of the 5th Workshop on Automated Knowledge Base Construction, pp. 35-39.

Lehnert, W. G. (1981). Plot units and narrative summarization. Cognitive science, 5(4), pp. 293-331.

Liu, J., Shang, J., Wang, C., Ren, X., & Han, J. (2015). Mining quality phrases from massive text corpora. In Proceedings of the 2015 ACM SIGMOD International Conference on Management of Data, pp. 1729-1744.

Maddela, M., Xu, W., & Preoţiuc-Pietro, D. (2019). Multi-task pairwise neural ranking for hashtag segmentation. arXiv preprint arXiv:1906.00790.

McClosky, D., Surdeanu, M., & Manning, C. D. (2011). Event extraction as dependency parsing for bionlp 2011. In Proceedings of the BioNLP Shared Task 2011 Workshop. Association for Computational Linguistics, pp. 41-45.

Miller, B. (2018). Cross-document narrative alignment of environmental news: A position paper on the challenge of using event chains to proxy narrative features. In Proceedings of the Workshop Events and Stories in the News 2018, pp. 18-24.

Ritter, A., Clark, S., & Etzioni, O. (2011). Named entity recognition in tweets: an experimental study. In Proceedings of the conference on empirical methods in natural language processing. Association for Computational Linguistics, pp. 1524-1534.

Reschke, K., Jankowiak, M., Surdeanu, M., Manning, C. D., & Jurafsky, D. (2014). Event extraction using distant supervision. In Proceedings of the International Conference on Language Resources and Evaluation Conference (LREC), pp4527-4531.

Vashishth, S., Jain, P., & Talukdar, P. (2018). Cesi: Canonicalizing open knowledge bases using embeddings and side information. In Proceedings of the 2018 World Wide Web Conference, pp. 1317-1327.

Wang, W. (2018). Event detection and extraction from news articles (Doctoral dissertation, Virginia Tech).

Wu, F., & Weld, D. S. (2010). Open information extraction using Wikipedia. In Proceedings of the 48th Annual Meeting of the Association for Computational Linguistics. Association for Computational Linguistics, pp. 118-127.

Yarlott, W. V. H., & Finlayson, M. A. (2016). Learning a better motif index: Toward automated motif extraction. In 7th Workshop on Computational Models of Narrative (CMN 2016).

9. Appendix A: 57 White Helmets Narratives

Narrative Tag	Description
israel_evac_wh	discusses event of Israel evacuating WH
wh_save_lives	author believes WH save peoples lives
wh_in_danger	WH are under threat or are deliberately targeted by Assad military, WH need to be rescued
wh_fake_evidence	WH stage videos or photos, or otherwise provide fake evidence
us_funding_freeze	discussion of event of US freezing WH funding
wh_terrorists	WH are linked to terrorists, help

	terrorists, or share facilities/resources with terrorists
uk_asylum	Discussion of event of UK providing asylum to WH members
uk_connection	WH connection to the UK by funding, policy, or official statements
us_connection	WH connection to the US by funding, policy, or official statements
russia_assad_connection	Russia and Assad act as a coordinated axis (negative)
civilian_casualties	Deaths of civilians during military actions by Russia or Assad gov
anti_wh_smear_campaign	WH are being targeted by misinfo or smear campaign
wh_propaganda	WH are propaganda tools or make propaganda
western_connection	WH are connected to "the west", NATO, or the EU, or are favored by "western" entities
wh_used_to_promote_regime_change	WH are a tool used to promote a "regime change" agenda
netherlands_funding_freeze	Discussion of Netherlands freezing funding for WH
russia_opposes_wh	Russia opposes the WH either in general or in a way distinct from a smear campaign
israel_connection	WH connection to Israel or "zionism" by funding, policy, or official statements
wh_participate_in_execution	WH participate in, are present during, or clean up after executions
wh_committed_war_crimes	WH committed mass murder or otherwise broke international law in violent ways
wh_not_legitimate	WH are a "fake" or "illegitimate" group or are contrasted with Assad government affiliated groups
media_favor_wh	Media outlets are biased in favor of wh, are complicit in falsifying evidence, or refuse to convey anti-WH information
wh_win_oscar	Discusses WH winning Oscar or refers to them as "oscar-winning"
wh_evac	Discussion of wh evacuation in general without mentioning Israel
wh_asylum	wh will be provided asylum or resettled in nonspecific country
wh_not_helpful	WH do not help civilians or do not accomplish what they claim
assad_war_crimes	Assad military actions are mass murder or other very violent acts
canada_asylum	WH are provided with asylum in Canada
covert_ops	WH are involved in covert operations or are secretly affiliated with foreign military or intelligence agencies
wh_foreign_influence	WH are affiliated with governments or organizations foreign to Syria, which makes them illegitimate.
germany_asylum	WH will be provided asylum in Germany
roger_waters_emails	Discussion of emails sent to Roger Waters requesting he endorse the WH, and his statements after that
wh_illegal_acts	WH engage in other heinous acts such as kidnapping, drugging people, or mishandling dead bodies
wh_organs	WH are organ traffickers or harvest organs of dead or living people
wh_document_crimes	WH provide video or photo evidence of war crimes by Russia or Assad
misinformation	Discussion of mis/disinformation

	or fake news as opposed to "smear campaign" which makes no claims of misinformation
official_hearings	Official hearings on the WH at the UN or at the Hague
france_connection	WH connected to French government
chemical_weapons	Discusses use of chemical weapons by Assad or Russia
censorship	Claims of censorship by YouTube, twitter for anti-WH statements
wh_weapons	Claims WH have weapons such as guns or bombs
elie_wiesel_award	WH win Elie Wiesel award
exposing_truth	Vague general statements about exposing lies or truth
wh_member_deaths	Statements paying respect to dead members of the WH
nobel_prize	WH nomination for nobel peace prize
events_pro_assad	General descriptions of events from a pro-Assad stance
anti_wh_campaign_interests_conspiracists	States that the anti-WH campaign is generally aligned with other conspiracy theories
critique_israel	Criticizes other Israeli actions in Gaza, etc.
general_anti_wh	Generally negative toward WH without clarification
jo_cox	Discussion of politician Jo Cox, who supported WH
james_le_mesurier	Discussion of WH founder with ties to UK
wh_threat_to_host	WH are a threat to host countries where they will be relocated
russia_wants_peace	Russia is faced with NATO aggression and is attempting to promote peace
canada_connection	WH is connected to Canadian government
wh_misc_positive	Miscellaneous positive statements or positive discussion of secondary WH programs
qanon	QAnon US politics (deep state, conspiracies, etc)
unrelated	False positive in data collection (e.g. Football team white helmets)

Proceedings of the Workshop on Social Threats in Online Conversations: Understanding and Management (STOC-2020), pages 48–55
Language Resources and Evaluation Conference (LREC 2020), Marseille, 11–16 May 2020

Email Threat Detection Using Distinct Neural Network Approaches

Esteban Castillo[1], Sreekar Dhaduvai[2], Peng Liu[2], Kartik-Singh Thakur[2], Adam Dalton[3] and Tomek Strzalkowski[1]
[1]Rensselaer Polytechnic Institute, Troy, NY, USA, {castie2, tomek}@rpi.edu
[2]State University of New York at Albany, Albany, NY, USA, {sdhaduvai, pliu3, kthakur}@albany.edu
[3]IHMC, Ocala, FL, USA, adalton@ihmc.us

Abstract

This paper describes different approaches to detect malicious content in email interactions through a combination of machine learning and natural language processing tools. Specifically, several neural network designs are tested on word embedding representations to detect suspicious messages and separate them from non-suspicious, benign email. The proposed approaches are trained and tested on distinct email collections, including datasets constructed from publicly available corpora (such as Enron, APWG, etc.) as well as several smaller, non-public datasets used in recent government evaluations. Experimental results show that back-propagation both with and without recurrent neural layers outperforms current state of the art techniques that include supervised learning algorithms with stylometric elements of texts as features. Our results also demonstrate that word embedding vectors are effective means for capturing certain aspects of text meaning that can be teased out through machine learning in non-linear/complex neural networks, in order to obtain highly accurate detection of malicious emails based on email text alone.

1. Introduction

Email messages are the dominant way of communication for many users around the world (Dada et al., 2019). Among the massive daily email traffic, unsolicited and unwanted messages[1] have become a growing nuisance and increasingly posing serious threats to users' privacy and security by distributing false information, deceptive requests, as well as malicious links and attachments.

A number of approaches have been used for detection and removal of malicious messages from email feeds (Mujtaba et al., 2017). For example, extraction of harmful content (payload) has solved many obvious problems, as did the analysis of email headers for sender addresses and delivery paths, but most of these techniques fail to understand the content of the message itself: does the message contain a request (explicit or implicit) for the addressee to perform an action that would harm them or their organization, e.g., by divulging private information? In other words, the message itself, and not necessarily any associated metadata, becomes a threat because it attempts to break the last line of defense: the user.

Given the challenging nature of the task, we propose a novel technique to identify suspicious emails based on the analysis of email textual content. *Our main contribution* is the evaluation of multiple neural network architectures applied to pre-trained word embedding representation to automatically acquire accurate indicators of malicious emails. *The papers main hypothesis* is that different non-linear models (neural networks architectures) can learn hidden correlations between text elements (represented as word embeddings) that are characteristic of malicious messages and do so more reliably than classic supervised learning approaches (bag of words, TD-IDF etc.). *Our motivation* is to create reliable content-based models that can classify email and other types of messages (such as SMS) as suspicious (spam, phishing, malware, propaganda, etc.) as a first line of defense against social engineering attacks (Sawa et al., 2016).

The remainder of this paper is organized as follows: in Section 2. current approaches to detection of suspicious email are reviewed. Sections 3. to 6. provide details of our design and implementation of the neural network architectures. In Section 7. the experimental results are presented and discussed. Finally, implications and conclusions derived from this work thus far are discussed in Section 8..

2. Related Work

In this section, we briefly review the most relevant recent work in the email analysis and classification, specifically those that use machine learning, highlighting their main features and performance.

(Diale et al., 2019) implemented a Support Vector Machine (SVM), Random Forest and decision tree algorithms for spam detection with a vector size reduction approach to eliminate excessive number of features. A distributed bag of words representation was used for fixed length embedding of email samples. Dimensionality reduction was utilized to capture word ordering and basic semantic meaning from text messages. Experimental results show an overall spam detection accuracy of 97% over the Enron dataset.

(Abu-Nimeh et al., 2007) compares distinct supervised learning algorithms (logistic regression, random forest, SVM, etc.) for detecting phishing emails. The approach considers a bag of words model as text representation with TF-IDF weights for detecting best features in the body of emails. Experimental results show an average accuracy of 92% over a manually annotated phishing dataset and identify the logistic regression and SVM algorithms as best options when text frequency distributions are analyzed.

(Abiodun et al., 2019) used a SVM and Naïve Bayes algorithm alongside a feature analysis process to detect phishing messages. Multiple content and header features were considered incrementally in order to find the optimal set of features that maximizes classification accuracy. Experimental

[1] Social engineering attacks, spam, phishing, malware, propaganda among others.

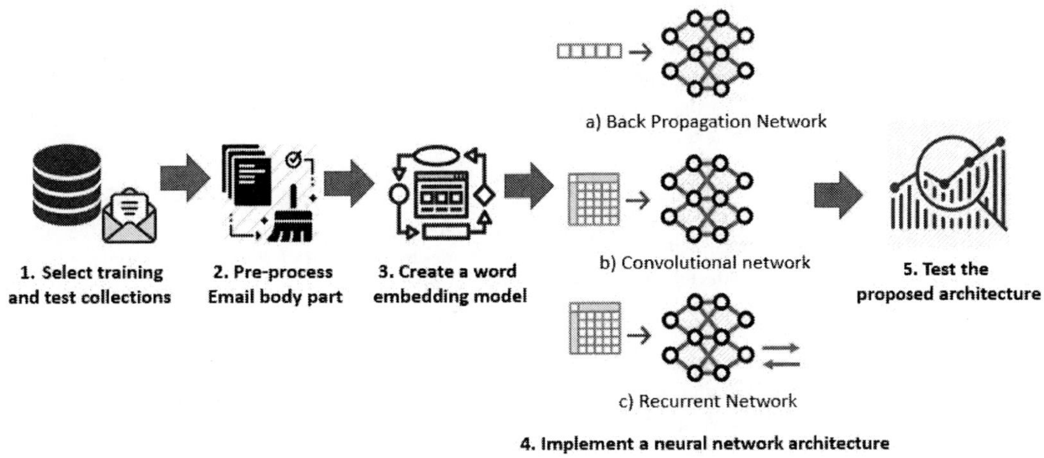

Figure 1: Email threat detection process.

results show accuracy around 98% for detecting phishing texts over messages that contain a verified set of phishing messages and URLs reported by volunteers (Alexa and PhishTank[2] collections).

(Varol and Abdulhadi, 2018) presented an heuristic spam filtering approach in which different string matching metrics (Levenshtein Edit-Distance, Longest Common Subsequence, etc.) are used to compare email text sentences over manually selected phrases related to spam and propaganda. Emails are labelled as friend or foe if most comparisons surpass a predefined numeric threshold. Experiments were run against the Enron and CSDMC2010 datasets showing spam detection accuracy around 98%.

(Bahgat et al., 2018) employed several supervised learning algorithms (SVM, Bayesian Logistic Regression) alongside an ontology and text similarity measures for detecting malicious email messages (spam and propaganda). The proposed approach employs the WordNet ontology to eliminate words with a similar meaning, then benign/non-benign emails are compared between each other using string matching measures where emails are label as foe if are similar to many malicious messages. Experimental results show an accuracy above 90% over the Enron dataset.

Finally, (M et al., 2018) describes a set of experiments for detecting phishing on emails by using a convolutional neural network with a word embedding approach over email headers or the messages itself (payload). The experiments obtained an accuracy around 96% which shows the importance of neural networks for detecting malicious attacks and demonstrate that word embeddings are a suitable for detecting fine-grained patterns of users writing style. Important to mentioned that this paper helps to see that a single model over spam, phishing, malware, etc. could be created by using word embedding and neural networks as platform.

Most of the above approaches work reasonably well, although some recent experiments using neural networks (Smadi et al., 2018; Roy et al., 2020) have been more successful, especially for generalizing models across different threat types and associated topics.

3. Threat Detection Process

In this section we discuss several variants of a new method for detecting multiple forms of malicious email that include phishing, spam, malware, propaganda, and also sophisticated forms of social engineering. Our method is tested on email, but it is general enough to apply to other types of messaging, including social media private messaging and chat channels. Figure 1 shows the overall approach with three alternative training modes with different neural network architectures. The process is explained below:

1. Select appropriate email collections for training and testing of the prediction models (see Section 4.).
2. Pre-process textual information in the body of emails. This task includes word tokenization, elimination of punctuation and special symbols, and converting all text to lowercase.
3. Create word embedding models taking as input all training email collections (see Section 5.).
4. Implement a neural network architecture that takes word embeddings obtained in the previous step as input and learns to classify emails into friend/foe or (in future experiments) more categories (e.g., friend, foe, undecided; as well as subtypes of foe messages) (see Section 6.).
5. Evaluate the trained models using set-aside test collections (see Section 7.).

4. Datasets Used

The document collections used for training and testing include benign and malicious email samples obtained from employees of public companies and government departments.

Benign emails correspond to internal interactions among users on day-to-day work issues. On the other hand, most of

[2] https://www.phishtank.com/

suspicious emails are obtained from employees spam boxes and specific email threat repositories (like APWG dataset). All emails have been manually labeled at source following the conventions of the data providers. For training purposes we converted these into binary suspicious/non-suspicious labels, but also kept the original labels as additional features (threat type).

In this application we only consider the (textual) body of emails; header and other metadata was not used.[3]. We also note that all personally identifiable information (PII) has been removed or replaced in the data. Attachments are kept in most cases, but these containing malware are eliminated to protect users.

Table 1 summarizes the key details of each collection. Enron and APWG (among other collections) are used for training purposes while Non-public datasets called dry-run 1 and dry-run 2 are used for testing.

Dataset name and/or type	Feature	Training	Testing
Enron	Used for word embeddings	✓	
(Klimt and Yang, 2004)	Collection type	Public available	
Benign emails	Number of emails	84111	NA
APWG (Oest et al., 2018)	Used for word embeddings	✓	
Phishing/Malware	Collection type	Public available	
Non-benign emails	Number of emails	30776	NA
BC3	Used for word embeddings	✓	
(Ulrich et al., 2008)	Collection type	Public available	
Benign emails	Number of emails	259	NA
Phishing[4]/non-phishing	Used for word embeddings	✓	
	Collection type	Non-public available	
Non-benign emails	Number of emails	5338	NA
Malware[5]/non-malware	Used for word embeddings	✓	
	Collection type	Non-public available	
Non-benign emails	Number of emails	2914	NA
Propaganda[6]	Used for word embeddings	✓	
/non-propaganda	Collection type	Non-public available	
Non-benign emails	Number of emails	261	NA
Spam[7]/non-spam	Used for word embeddings	✓	
	Collection type	Non-public available	
Non-benign emails	Number of emails	1294	NA
social engineering[8]	Used for word embeddings	✓	
/non-social engineering	Collection type	Non-public available	
Non-benign emails	Number of emails	1059	NA
Reconnaissance[9]	Used for word embeddings	✓	
/non-reconnaissance	Collection type	Non-public available	
Non-benign emails	Number of emails	173	NA
Dry-run 1	Used for word embeddings	✗	
Benign and	Collection type	Non-public available	
Non-benign emails	Number of emails	NA	1025
Dry-run 2	Used for word embeddings	✗	
Benign and	Collection type	Non-public available	
Non-benign emails	Number of emails	NA	3023

Table 1: Datasets used in this study.

From above table, it is important to highlight that dry-run datasets comprise also email samples of day-to-day interactions in a work environment. This collections are non public available considering that there are utilize for evaluating an active social engineering program of the USA government. Despite that, it can be mentioned that this datasets have an unbalanced nature with a proportion of 80% benign samples and 20% non-benign ones which is consistent with a real world scenario.

5. Word Embeddings

Accurate detection of suspicious emails in the stream of daily messages, based on email content alone, requires attention to subtle differences in word use, sequencing, and the "tone" of the message. Unlike most ordinary communication, malicious messages attempt to produce a reaction from the recipient in a manner that tends to violate communication norms – the subtleties that we are attempting to tease out.

Word embeddings (Mikolov et al., 2013; Bengio et al., 2006) which capture contextual meaning of words in texts by creating vector representations, are particularly suitable for this task. We derive word embeddings from a corpus of emails, thus capturing what we believe are the contextual meanings of words use in email genre.

In this paper, a continuous bag-of-word model based on Gensim-word2vec (Řehůřek and Sojka, 2010) is utilized for obtaining numerical vectors of words. We use a window of 10 words for analyzing the neighborhood of texts and vectors of different size are created for testing different neural networks architectures (see Section 7.1.).

In the next section we explain the role of word embedding vectors as inputs to a supervised learning algorithm implemented with different neural network architectures.

6. Neural Networks Architectures

Neural networks (Goodfellow et al., 2016) are a special type of classifiers which are strongly tied to supervised machine learning suitable for modeling of non-linear problems.

Figure 2 shows the three neural network architectures proposed for training classifiers for suspicious/non-suspicious emails. All variants are implemented in Keras (Chollet, 2017) as follows:

1. **Back-propagation network**: A classic feed-forward network which creates multiple hidden layers between input and output elements. This architecture adjusts model efficiency according to a gradient descent technique (Ruder, 2016) which minimizes the error rate after multiple back and forth iterations over the network on training samples.

   Figure 3a highlights how the word embeddings are utilized as input in the back-propagation process. For each training and test emails, content word embedding vectors are combined into a single vector by computing averages across corresponding dimensions. The objective is to obtain a vector representing the meaning of each email.

2. **Convolutional network**: A specialization of the back-propagation model (Indolia et al., 2018) that employs mathematical transformations (convolutions)

[3] Header information included in the emails is not always complete due to privacy considerations.

[4] Email messages often used to steal users data.

[5] Emails embedded code designed to cause extensive damage to users data/systems.

[6] Email sent to disseminate facts, arguments, rumours related to a specific topic.

[7] Unsolicited, undesired or annoying email messages.

[8] Email message used for manipulate users, so they give up confidential information voluntarily.

[9] Email sent to gain preliminary information about a potential victim.

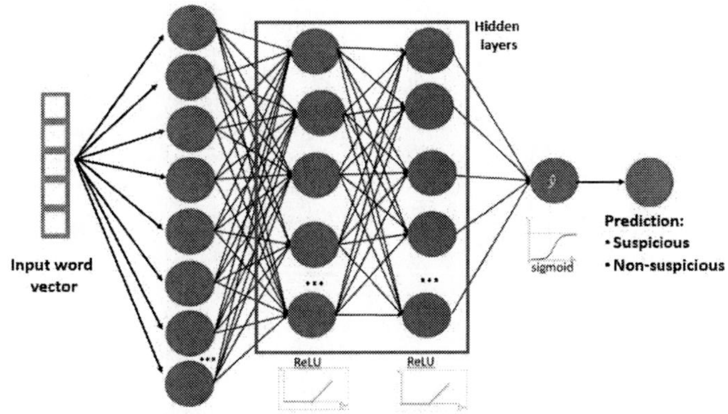

(a) Back-propagation network.

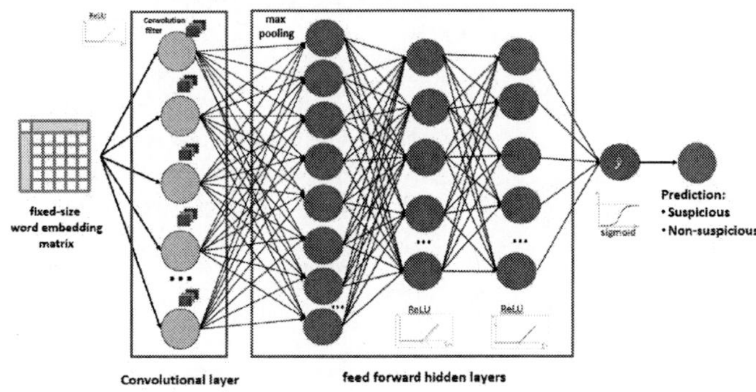

(b) Convolutional network.

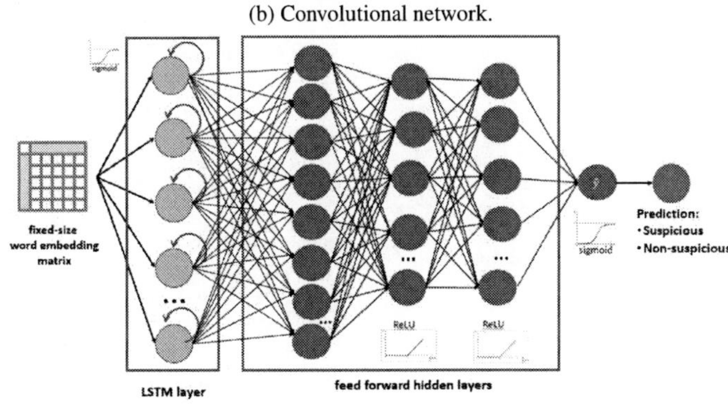

(c) Recurrent network (LSTM).

Figure 2: Proposed neural network architectures.

over specific hidden layers for detecting fine grained features. The combined new features (max pooling), help capturing patterns related to order and proximity over the words, increasing the detection of spatio-temporal aspects of original texts.

Figure 3b shows how the embeddings are used in this architecture. A fixed-size matrix is created for each training and test email taking as input tokens from text. In this matrix, columns represent features of an embedding vector and rows represent tokens associated with email samples.

It is important to note that this type of architecture requires matrices of the same size. Accordingly, we take the first N words from each email as input to the process[10].

3. **Recurrent neural network**: Another specialization of back-propagation model (Hochreiter and Schmidhuber, 1997; Soutner and Müller, 2013) where data sequences are analyzed in order to predict new ones based on prior knowledge. In this architecture, specific hidden layers implement neuron loops allowing a small memory state where previous words are used as input to current word analysis, this help to relate token patterns that are syntactically separate in the word

[10] If an email is shorter than N, all its words are used as rows in a matrix and the remaining positions are padded with zeros.

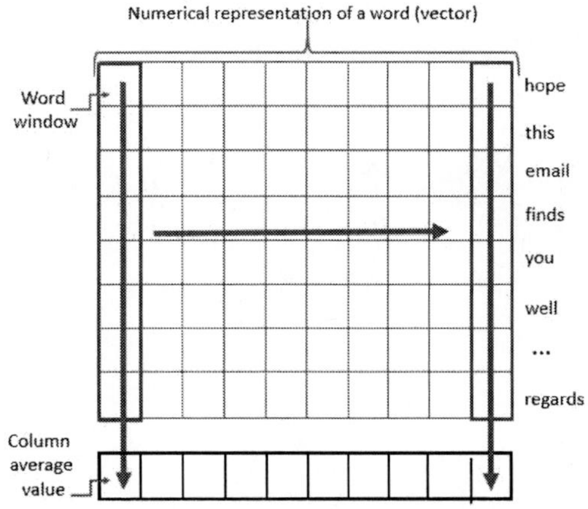

(a) Back-propagation network.

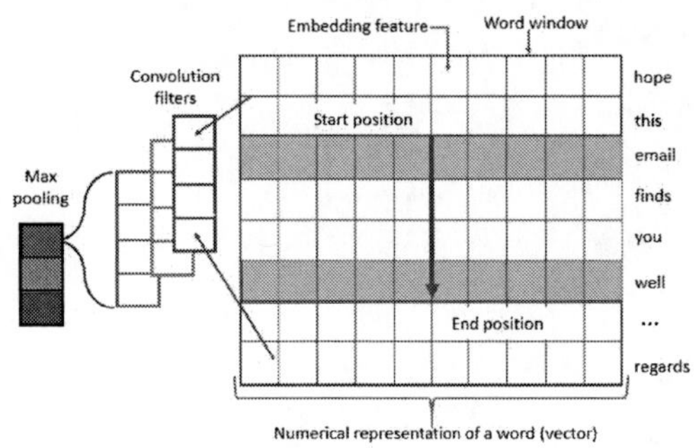

(b) Convolutional network.

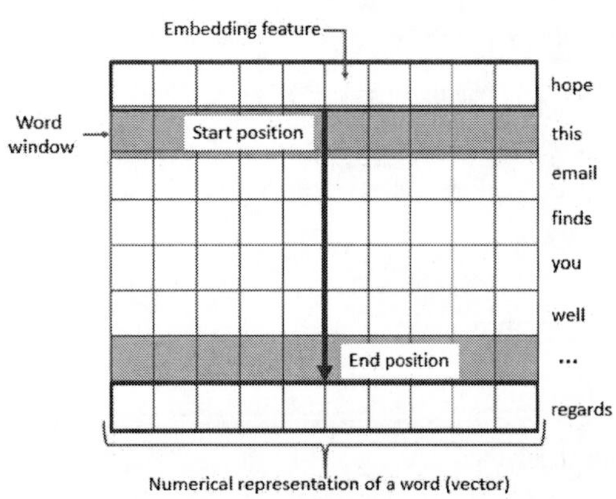

(c) LSTM network.

Figure 3: Word embedding matrix representations.

sequence.

In this paper, we used a specific type of recurrent network called Long Short-Term Memory network (LSTM). This kind of network expands the idea of a memory state by creating a complex architecture of nodes that remember information of correlated elements that are far away (key difference from a classical recurrent network). LSTM networks analyze and predict information considering past knowledge, which most of the time is omitted or managed independently introducing some bias to the learning algorithms.

Figure 3c show how the LSTM network takes consecutive word windows in order to analyze past, present and future words in the email text. As with the convolutional network, LSTMs require inputs of the same size, therefore only the first N email words are used as input in the network.

7. Experimental Results

Results obtained using the proposed neural network architectures are discussed in this section. First, the experiments are described, then the results are shown, and followed by a discussion of the findings.

7.1. Experiments Performed

A series of experiments were performed in order to test the accuracy of the proposed variants. In total, 60480 experimental runs were performed using multiple combinations of neural network parameters for each architecture type. Table 2 summarizes the different configurations that were tested in a **supervised learning** fashion.

Parameter	Possible values
Programming language	Python https://www.python.org/
Neural network package	Keras https://keras.io/
Word embedding package	Gensim https://radimrehurek.com/gensim/
Email words/tokens (Matrix rows)	$10, 20, 30, 40$
Word embedding features (Matrix columns)	$30, 40, 50, 60$
Convolutional layer (number of neurons)	$20, 30, 40, 50$
LSTM layer (number of neurons)	$30, 40, 50, 60$
Back-propagation neurons (Multiple hidden layers)	50-50,32-16-8-3,8-8,4-4,3-3-3
Convolutional word window	3
LSTM word window	2
Convolutional network filter number	100
Convolutional activation function	Relu
LSTM activation function	Sigmoid
Back-propagation activation function	Relu and Sigmoid
Batches	$50, 60, 70, 80, 90, 100, 110$
Epochs	$2, 3, 4, 5, 6, 7$

Table 2: Experimental parameters.

It is worth noting that parameters were selected according to a preliminary experimentation and the recommendations from relevant literature (Lane et al., 2019).

7.2. Experimental Results

Table 3 summarizes the results over dry-run 1 and dry-run 2 test collections. Experimental results obtained from variants of NN architecture, as explained above, are compared against traditional classifiers (SVM, NB, and LR) that use

Dataset type	Approach	Features (Matrix colums)	Email length (Matrix rows)	LSTM Neurons	Convolutional Neurons	Back-Propagation Neurons	Batches	Epochs	Accuracy
Dry-Run 1	BP	60	40	–	–	8-8	70	6	**0.9568***
	LSTM	50	40	50	–	32-16-8-3	90	7	0.9317
	BP	50	50	–	–	4-4	100	6	0.9127
	CN	20	40	–	40	8-8	50	4	0.9175
	LSTM	30	50	60	–	4-4	110	6	0.9114
	BP	40	40	–	–	8-8	90	5	0.9031
	BP	30	60	–	–	8-8	50	4	0.9012
	LSTM	40	40	50	–	32-16-8-3	60	6	0.8855
	LSTM	40	50	60	–	50-50	90	7	0.8821
	CN	20	30	–	40	3-3-3	60	4	0.8793
	SVM	–	–	–	–	–	–	–	0.8137
	NB	–	–	–	–	–	–	–	0.7915
	LR	–	–	–	–	–	–	–	0.7824
Dry-Run 2	LSTM	30	40	60	–	3-3-3	60	5	**0.9185***
	BP	40	60	–	–	8-8	70	7	0.9136
	BP	30	60	–	–	3-3-3	80	5	0.9023
	BP	40	40	–	–	4-4	70	6	0.9012
	CN	20	30	–	40	50-50	50	3	0.8983
	BP	30	40	–	–	32-16-8-3	70	4	0.8839
	CN	30	30	–	40	32-16-8-3	50	3	0.8748
	LSTM	40	50	60	–	8-8	100	6	0.8612
	SVM	–	–	–	–	–	–	–	0.8529
	BP	40	40	–	–	50-50	110	6	0.8512
	BP	30	30	–	–	3-3-3	80	5	0.8507
	LR	–	–	–	–	–	–	–	0.8045
	NB	–	–	–	–	–	–	–	0.7749

BP: Back-propagation
CN: Convolutional Network
LSTM: Long Short-Term Memory Network (recurrent network)
SVM: Support Vector Machine
NB: Naïve Bayes
LR: Logistic Regression

Table 3: Summary of best experimental results.

standard bag of words approach[11] (Manning et al., 2008; Sarah Guido, 2016).

Experimental results demonstrate that the performance of all neural network variants surpasses baseline techniques using three main options with customized word embeddings over dry-run 1 and 2: back-propagation accuracy (95%, 91%), convolutional network accuracy (91%, 89%) and LSTM network accuracy (93%, 91%).

The best results (independently of the test collection) were obtained using the first 30 to 40 words of each email, which indicates that the core threat information is included in this range. For the word embeddings size, relatively small vectors of 40 to 60 features appear to pack the semantic content of emails to capture the distinctive indicators associated with email intent (malicious or benign).

The major advantage of the LSTM and convolutional networks is the fine grained analysis of word sequences, which helps to identify subtle textual patterns that are lost when each word is considered independently. On the other hand, the major disadvantage is the extra amount of time and resources required for training for relatively modest performance gain.

Finally, the obtained results demonstrate that the proposed neural network configurations can be used to effectively train accurate classifiers for detecting suspicious emails independently of their topic and subject domain. This fact highlights the relevance of the neural networks created and the features used as an effective method of capturing the intent of emails.

8. Conclusions and Future Work

Several neural network architectures were tested in order to train effective classifiers for identification of malicious content in email messages, independently of their subject matter. The results demonstrate viability of the proposed methods for capturing malicious intent in messages. Our key findings are summarized below:

1. *Datasets* selected for this project are shown to be relevant for training and testing the email classifiers. Taken together, they provide sufficient lexical and syntactic resources for effective learning of textual patterns related to malicious messages.

2. *Word embeddings* proved to be an adequate option for representing the writing style of malicious emails. This technique helped to capture the context of words in email messages as well as their relationship with other words which ultimately lead to an accurate representation.

3. The *back-propagation network* obtained the best results compared with other approaches. This highlights the ability of the model to learn non-linear and complex relationships between inputs and outputs. Results

[11] Baseline experiments were implemented using the whole set of words on the training collections as features and the default parameters for the scikit-learn package for classifiers.

obtained also demonstrate that the analysis of dense feed forward networks helps to generalize textual patterns across multiple email threat types.

4. The *convolutional networks* achieved a performance slightly below baseline results. This reveals that convolutions over word embeddings windows of size up to three are not enough to fully capture the writing style of malicious email messages. A higher accuracy could be obtained if complete word embedding windows are analyzed although it would consume a higher number of computational resources due to the complexity of the network.

5. The *recurrent neural networks* obtained similar results than baseline techniques. The results demonstrate that the analysis of words that are dependent of previous ones is not crucial for detecting suspicious email messages independently of the threat type.

6. Overall, our results surpass baseline techniques showing the relevance of the neural networks approach combined with word embeddings for detecting distinctive elements on email exchanges. Results also show the effectiveness of the networks in a real world application (Non-public datasets) where emails could not be related to the topics and domains used for training.

Future work includes the following actions:

- Run related work methods (see Section 2.) against test collections used in this paper (dry-run 1 and 2). The idea is to compare state of the art accuracy associated to a specific threat type (spam, or phishing) with the results obtained in this paper where classifier created can deal with different types of threats.
- Add more public email samples that deal with the problem in order to enrich the training process over the neural network architectures that show a better performance.
- Refine and enrich existing training datasets by careful manual labelling by multiple annotators.
- Apply additional neural networks techniques (Chollet, 2017; Lane et al., 2019) for improving the approach accuracy.
- Evaluate the proposed approach on different genre of messaging, e.g. social media channels (Inuwa-Dutse et al., 2018).
- Apply this approach in other languages (e.g., Spanish) keeping the same neural network parameters but creating a new word embedding model according to the language vocabulary.

Acknowledgments

Supported by DARPA FA8650-18-C-7881 and by DARPA through Army Contract W31P4Q-17-C-0066. All statements are those of the authors, not AFRL, DARPA, Army, or USG.

9. Bibliographical References

Abiodun, O., Sodiya, A., and Akinwale, A. T. (2019). A predictive model for phishing detection. *Journal of King Saud University - Computer and Information Sciences*, 1:1–16.

Abu-Nimeh, S., Nappa, D., Wang, X., and Nair, S. (2007). A comparison of machine learning techniques for phishing detection. In *Proceedings of the Anti-Phishing Working Groups 2nd Annual ECrime Researchers Summit*, page 60–69. Association for Computing Machinery.

Bahgat, E. M., Rady, S., Gad, W., and Moawa, I. F. (2018). Efficient email classification approach based on semantic methods. *Ain Shams Engineering Journal*, 9(4):3259 – 3269.

Bengio, Y., Schwenk, H., Senécal, J.-S., Morin, F., and Gauvain, J.-L., (2006). *Neural Probabilistic Language Models*, pages 137–186. Springer Berlin Heidelberg, Berlin, Heidelberg.

Chollet, F., (2017). *Deep Learning with Python*, pages 178–232. Manning Publications Co., Shelter Island, NY 11964.

Dada, E. G., Bassi, J. S., Chiroma, H., Abdulhamid, S. M., Adetunmbi, A. O., and Ajibuwa, O. E. (2019). Machine learning for email spam filtering: review, approaches and open research problems. *Heliyon*, 5(6):1–23.

Diale, M., Celik, T., and Walt, C. V. D. (2019). Unsupervised feature learning for spam email filtering. *Computers & Electrical Engineering*, 74:89–104.

Goodfellow, I., Bengio, Y., and Courville, A. (2016). *Deep Learning*. MIT Press, Cambridge, Massachusetts.

Hochreiter, S. and Schmidhuber, J. (1997). Long short-term memory. *Neural Computation*, 9(8):1735–1780.

Indolia, S., Goswami, A. K., Mishra, S. P., and Asopa, P. (2018). Conceptual understanding of convolutional neural network- a deep learning approach. *Procedia Computer Science*, 132:679–688.

Inuwa-Dutse, I., Liptrott, M., and Korkontzelos, I. (2018). Detection of spam-posting accounts on twitter. *Neurocomputing*, 315:496–511.

Klimt, B. and Yang, Y. (2004). The enron corpus: A new dataset for email classification research. In *Machine Learning: ECML 2004*, pages 217–226. Springer Berlin Heidelberg.

Lane, H., Howard, C., and Hapke, H., (2019). *Natural Language Processing in Action*, pages 247–273. Manning Publications Co., Shelter Island, NY 11964.

M, H., Unnithan, N. A., R, V., and Kp, S. (2018). Deep learning based phishing e-mail detection cen-deepspam. In *1st AntiPhishing Shared Pilot 4th ACM Int. Workshop Secur. Privacy Anal.(IWSPA)*, pages 1–5.

Manning, C. D., Raghavan, P., and Schütze, H., (2008). *Introduction to Information Retrieval*, pages 18–43. Cambridge University Press.

Mikolov, T., Sutskever, I., Chen, K., Corrado, G., and Dean, J. (2013). Distributed representations of words and phrases and their compositionality. In *Proceedings of the 26th International Conference on Neural Information Processing Systems - Volume 2*, pages 3111–3119. Curran Associates Inc.

Mujtaba, G., Shuib, L., Raj, R. G., Majeed, N., and Al-Garadi, M. A. (2017). Email classification research trends: Review and open issues. *IEEE Access*, 5:9044–9064.

Oest, A., Safei, Y., Doupe, A., Ahn, G.-J., Wardman, B., and Warner, G. (2018). Inside a phisher's mind: Understanding the anti-phishing ecosystem through phishing kit analysis. In *Proceedings of the 2018 APWG Symposium on Electronic Crime Research, eCrime 2018*, pages 1–12. IEEE Computer Society.

Řehůřek, R. and Sojka, P. (2010). Software framework for topic modelling with large corpora. In *Proceedings of the LREC 2010 Workshop on New Challenges for NLP Frameworksg*, pages 45–50. ELRA.

Roy, P. K., Singh, J. P., and Banerjee, S. (2020). Deep learning to filter sms spam. *Future Generation Computer Systems*, 102:524–533.

Ruder, S. (2016). An overview of gradient descent optimization algorithms. *CoRR*, abs/1609.04747:1–14.

Sarah Guido, A. M., (2016). *Introduction to Machine Learning with Python*, pages 27–129. O'Reilly Media.

Sawa, Y., Bhakta, R., Harris, I. G., and Hadnagy, C. (2016). Detection of social engineering attacks through natural language processing of conversations. In *2016 IEEE Tenth International Conference on Semantic Computing (ICSC)*, pages 262–265. IEEE.

Smadi, S., Aslam, N., and Zhang, L. (2018). Detection of online phishing email using dynamic evolving neural network based on reinforcement learning. *Decision Support Systems*, 107:88–102.

Soutner, D. and Müller, L. (2013). Application of lstm neural networks in language modelling. In *Text, Speech, and Dialogue*, pages 105–112. Springer Berlin Heidelberg.

Ulrich, J., Murray, G., , and Carenini, G. (2008). A publicly available annotated corpus for supervised email summarization. In *AAAI08 EMAIL Workshop*, pages 1–6. AAAI.

Varol, C. and Abdulhadi, H. M. T. (2018). Comparision of string matching algorithms on spam email detection. In *2018 International Congress on Big Data, Deep Learning and Fighting Cyber Terrorism (IBIGDELFT)*, pages 6–11.

Association for Computational Linguistics
209 N. Eighth Street
Stroudsburg, Pennsylvania 18360

ISBN 978-1-7138-1278-4

CURRAN ASSOCIATES INC.
proceedings.com